NEVER
EAT
SHREDDED
WHEAT

NEVER EAT SHREDDED WHEAT

Weird Ways to Remember Things

JAMES M. RUSSELL

Michael O'Mara Books Limited

First published in Great Britain in 2018 by
Michael O'Mara Books Limited
9 Lion Yard
Tremadoc Road
London SW4 7NQ

Picture credits: Clipart.com: pages 12, 17, 38, 44, 66, 67, 69, 82 (dog),
109; iStock: pages 21, 32, 34, 41, 60, 157; Illustration of Old St. Paul's
Cathedral in flames by Wenceslaus Hollar: page 28; Openclipart: page 26;
Shutterstock: pages 16, 39, 62, 64, 65, 68, 79, 82 (fox), 106, 162, 170, 181.

A CIP catalogue record for this book is available from the British Library.

Papers used by Michael O'Mara Books Limited are natural,
recyclable products made from wood grown in sustainable
forests. The manufacturing processes conform to the
environmental regulations of the country of origin.

ISBN: 978-1-78243-989-9 in hardback print format
ISBN: 978-1-78243-991-2 in ebook format

1 2 3 4 5 6 7 8 9 10

Designed and typeset by Tetragon, London

Printed and bound by CPI Group (UK) Ltd, Croydon, CR0 4YY

www.mombooks.com

CONTENTS

INTRODUCTION

The Memory Palace
Why Mnemonics Work

Our memories are mysterious things. At one moment we might remember a lengthy poem or the exact street address of a restaurant from our childhood. But at the next moment we can struggle to recall where we have put our keys down or the name of the person to whom we have just been introduced.

Since ancient times, people have looked for ways to improve or augment their memory. The Greek poet Simonides of Ceos is credited with developing the 'method of loci', a way of remembering complex lists of information by associating each item in the list with a particular location. This is the idea behind 'memory palaces', as featured in the well-known *Sherlock* TV series and used by many magicians, within which a galaxy of information can be stored by a practised user.

The point of a memory palace is that it can create an easy way to access a particular memory or piece of information. The human mind is not terribly good at remembering abstract data – however, we can do it much more successfully if we create associations with more relatable bits of information, such as familiar people, places, colours, poems or jokes.

The mnemonics that many of us learned as children are simply a shortcut to help locate information within your memory. For instance, rather than remember that the clockwise order of the points of the compass is North, East, South, West, we remember the mnemonic 'Never Eat Shredded Wheat', and the combination of humour and a visual reference provides an instant cue for our brains.

Similarly, to remember the months of the year that have particular numbers of days, we can simply remember the rhyme that starts 'Thirty days hath September ...'; to remember the order of the first four geological periods of the Earth, we might remember that 'Camels Order Silver Devices' and use that to reconstruct the correct order: Cambrian, Ordovician, Silurian, Devonian; you can use the mnemonic 'A Comfortable Cave Of Many Marvellous Ornaments' to help you avoid misspelling 'accommodate'; while salesmen might inspire themselves with the acronym ABC: 'Always Be Closing'. In each case it is easier to access information by using the memorable key first, and then using this to unlock the facts and figures we actually require.

This book is a cornucopia of mnemonics. It includes some well-known examples that you might remember from school, some of which have been in use for centuries, as well as more recent ones and alternatives to the traditional versions.

Ranging across history, science, language, numbers, business, art and much, much more, the mnemonics included here provide quick and easy access to a vast amount of fascinating and useful information. In addition, there are sections on working out your own methods and systems to augment the existing mnemonics with your own aides-memoire, which can help you with everyday tasks such as avoiding common misspellings or remembering names, faces and numbers.

Mnemonics can be amusing as well as informative. Hopefully, while you are browsing through the range of memory aids included here, you will be reminded of some of those fascinating facts you learned at school but can't quite remember, while also picking up a few new pieces of general knowledge and being entertained along the way.

IN THE
FIRST PLACE

Memory Methods
and Systems

The art of improving your memory is quite easy to explain. You simply need to take a piece of information, whether it be a list, name, number, word or face that you find hard to remember or fear you might forget. Then you associate this piece of information with something else that you find easier to remember. Then, when you need to access the difficult information, you use the easier information as the key for unlocking your memory.

Of course, that is easily said, but actually putting the idea into practice requires a range of strategies, which will come in useful in different situations. Here's a quick overview of the main strategies that are used in mnemonics and memory systems, all of which will be used at times in this book.

KEYWORDS

One of the simplest methods of remembering things is to use keywords. Imagine that you are learning French and want to remember the word for dragonfly: *libellule*. You might notice that the word contains the English word 'libel', which is easier for you to remember than the French word. Then, in order to create a connection between the two items, you could imagine a talking dragonfly spreading libellous rumours. Or, if you want to remember that the largest moon of Mars is called Phobos, you might imagine someone who is terrified of moons, and who therefore has a **phob**ia.

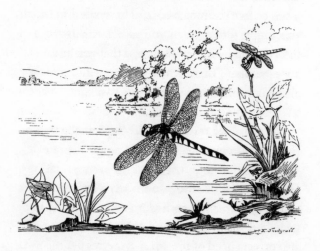

CHUNKING AND TRANSLATING

The human mind is especially bad at remembering long chains of information. For instance, we find it easier to remember the spelling of the short words 'flu', 'ore' and 'scent' than we do 'fluorescent', so knowing that the long word can be made up of the shorter words can help us to reconstruct the correct spelling. When it comes to numbers, we can use a similar process of 'chunking': for instance, we find it easier to remember the number 36254739958 as a series of shorter chunks 362 5473 9958. Long numbers are still quite difficult to remember, however, so it can be more effective to find ways to 'translate' numbers into verbal or visual images. We can, for instance, use the 'mnemonic major system', in which you replace each digit of the number with a letter and then turn the number into words (*see* pp. 42 and 43 for examples). Or we can use this letter-counting mnemonic to remember the speed of light:

> We guarantee certainty, clearly referring to this light mnemonic.

To translate this into a number, you count the number of letters in each word – 'we' has 2 letters, 'guarantee' has 9 letters, and so on – which gives us the correct speed of 299,792,458 metres per second.

MUSIC AND RHYME

Many people find it easier to remember information if it can be reshaped to fit a tune or to form a poem or rhyme. A recent campaign to persuade people to test their smoke alarms used the rhyme 'Press to test, Monthly is best' to try and impress on people's minds the importance of regularly checking the batteries. And generations of children have grown up with the ABC song, in which the alphabet is sung to the tune of 'Twinkle, Twinkle, Little Star'.

MAKING CONNECTIONS

It is always easier to remember a piece of information if you can make a visual connection. If, for instance, you meet someone called Dorothy Walker, and immediately bring to mind an image of Dorothy walking down the Yellow Brick Road, you are much more likely to remember her name than if you hadn't thought of that visual image. And in the dragonfly example above, you will be more likely to remember the libellous dragonfly if you actually picture it flitting around a specific pond with which you are familiar. Visual mnemonics can also be as simple as the example opposite, which is used in schools to teach the difference between 'their' and 'there'.

ACROSTICS AND ACRONYMS

Some of the most common mnemonics are acrostics and acronyms. In both cases, a list of words or a sentence is reduced to its capital letters (or a similarly reduced version). You get a plain acronym when you simply remember the capital letters. For instance, AAA could be used as an acronym for **A**crostics **A**nd **A**cronyms.

Acronyms are widely used for the names of organizations such as the Central Intelligence Agency – the CIA – and can also be used to remember lists and sentences, as in **KISS** for **K**eep **I**t **S**imple, **S**tupid. An acrostic is essentially a sentence that can be used to remember an acronym. For instance, the order of the first four planets from the Sun, **M**ercury, **V**enus, **E**arth and **M**ars, could be remembered with the acronym **MVEM**, but it is easier to remember **M**y **V**isitor **E**ats **M**ice, then convert this back into the acronym in order to access the correct order.

Acrostics are also widely used to
remember the spellings of tricky words,
for instance, to remember how to
spell **acrostic**:

A Curious Rabble Of Spanish
Tailors In Camisoles.

or

Anne Can Remember Obscure Spellings Terrific-
ally In Class.

MEMORY PALACES

The method of loci is a more organized way of using
visual connections to remember a list of information.
To use a memory palace, you pick a place or building
with which you are familiar, and then create visual
connections that you reinforce by placing them in
different 'locations'. Imagine, for instance, you are
using your local park as the memory palace, and you
want to remember this list of people you have just
met: Thomas is the salesperson, Eve is the manager
and Dave is the designer.

If you have decided to use the playground as the
first location, you might imagine Thomas sitting on

the swings selling a Thomas the Tank Engine toy. Then you could move on to Eve by the duckpond telling a snake with an apple what to do, and then Dave waving to someone while he is drawing in the café. The point is to find a way to create a visual association for each person that will give you clues to recreate the full list, so that you can then work your way back through the series of locations in the memory palace.

It is thought that the saying 'in the first place' comes from the use of the method of loci in the past: because the first thing you remember in a memory palace is the thing that is 'in the first place'.

PEG SYSTEMS

Peg memory systems are similar to memory palaces in that they use a set list of information with which you associate new information, but they work by associating particular numbers or words with a pre-learned list of images. For instance, if you have previously learned to associate the number 14 with a fireman and 23 with a giraffe, you might remember the number 1423 by picturing a fireman spraying a hose on a giraffe. (See page 43 for more on peg systems.)

STORIES

Some mnemonics work by telling a story or can be reinforced by the use of a narrative. For instance, the acrostic

> **H**appy **H**enry **L**ikes **B**eer **B**ut **C**ould **N**ot **O**rder
> **F**or **N**ine

is used to remember the first ten elements: Hydrogen, Helium, Lithium, Beryllium, Boron, Carbon, Nitrogen, Oxygen, Fluorine and Neon. You can further reinforce your ability to recall this story if you remember Happy Henry and his friends walking into a bar, in three rows of three people, and the barman refusing to serve him beer for them all.

DO-IT-YOURSELF

We've crammed as much as we can into this book, so you will find mnemonics here for a wide variety of information from history, medicine, geography, business and the arts to language and grammar. Do bear in mind, however, that there are many variations on these mnemonics, and the most effective method can be to make up your own new mnemonics. This can be fun and even more effective when it comes to fixing the information in your mind. So, it might be best to take this book both as a sourcebook of easy ways to remember stuff, and also as an inspiration to use mnemonics in your own life to remember everything from your daily shopping list to the names of your child's teachers to the names of your new colleagues.

REMEMBER, REMEMBER, THE FIFTH OF NOVEMBER

British History

The teaching of British history has changed somewhat in recent decades. There used to be more focus on long lists of monarchs and battles, whereas there is now more focus on industrial progress and social history. It can still be useful, however, to find ways to remember key dates and names across all areas of history. In this chapter we will take a look at some traditional mnemonics and rhymes as well as suggesting some new ones.

ANCIENT ERAS

If you need to remember the order of historical ages, you can start with this short rhyme for the Palaeolithic, Mesolithic, Neolithic, Bronze Age and Iron Age:

A **pale mes**s of **neo**n
Then **bronze** before **iron**.

For the predominant peoples of England (Celts, Roman, Saxon, Norman), you could use:

Clever **R**onaldo **S**aves **N**orway.

Or

Excellent **Je**rome **Sa**cks **Norma**.

THE ENGLISH CIVIL WAR

… Charles found the people a cruel corrector;
Oliver Cromwell was called Lord Protector …

In the following list of royal dynasties, you'll have noticed the eleven-year gap in the Stuart dynasty. This was, of course, due to the English Civil War, which ended with the execution of Charles I (as suggested in the rhyming couplet above). To simplify a long story, Britain was ruled by parliament from 1649 to 1660, with Oliver Cromwell (the 'OC', if you

ROYAL DYNASTIES

Here is a list of the royal dynasties from the Norman period onwards:

- **Norman** (1066–1154)
- **Plantagenet** (1154 –1399)
- **Lancaster** (1399–1461; 1470–1)
- **York** (1461–70, 1471–85)
- **Tudor** (1485–1603)
- **Stuart** (1603–49; 1660–1714)
- **Hanover** (1714–1901)
- **Saxe-Coburg-Gotha** (1901–17)
- **Windsor** (1917–to date)

The most commonly used mnemonics for this list are:

> **N**eighbours **P**ersuaded **L**ovely **Y**vonne **T**o **S**hut **H**er **S**ash **W**indow.

Or, if counting the Saxe-Coburgs as Windsors:

> **N**o **P**oint **L**etting **Y**our **T**rousers **S**lip **H**alf **W**ay.

struggle to remember his initials ...) in a dominant position up until his death in 1658. He was succeeded as 'Lord Protector' by his son Richard, who lacked authority and resigned, triggering the military skirmishes that led to the restoration of the monarchy.

The major battles of the Civil War were:

- Edgehill, 23 October 1642
- Adwalton Moor, 30 June 1643
- Roundway Down, 13 July 1643
- First Battle of Newbury, 20 September 1643
- Marston Moor, 2 July 1644
- Second Battle of Newbury, 27 October 1644
- Naseby, 14 June 1645

To remember the locations, you can use the mnemonic:

Each Afternoon, Run Nine Miles Nearly Naked.

For an account of the role of the Diggers in the Civil War, you may want to look up a folksong called 'The World Turned Upside Down', written by Leon Rosselson and covered by a variety of other artists. The version sung by both Dick Gaughan and Billy Bragg starts, 'In 1649, to St George's Hill, a ragged band they called the Diggers came, to show the people's will.' If nothing else it will help to fix the date of 1649, when King Charles I lost both his throne and his head, in your mind.

BRITISH KINGS AND QUEENS

There is a long traditional rhyme that records the kings and queens of England and (from the eighteenth century) the United Kingdom. It starts like this:

> Willie, Willie, Harry, Stee,
> Harry, Dick, John, Harry Three,
> One to Three Neds, Richard Two
> Harrys Four Five Six ... then who?
> Edwards Four Five, Dick the Bad,
> Harrys twain, Ned Six the lad,
> Mary, Bessie, James you ken,
> Then Charlie, Charlie, James again ...

Thus far in the rhyme, the list of monarchs is William I 'the Conqueror' (1066–87), William II 'Rufus' (1087–1100), Henry I (1100–35), Stephen (1135–54), Henry II (1154–89), Richard I 'the Lionheart' (1189–99), John (1199–1216), Henry III (1216–72), Edward I (1272–1307), Edward II (1307–27), Edward III (1327–77), Richard II (1377–1399), Henry IV (1399–1413), Henry V (1413–22), Henry VI (1422–61, 1470–1), Edward IV (1461–70, 1471–83), Edward V (1483), Richard III (1483–5), Henry VII (1485–1509), Henry VIII (1509–47), Edward VI (1547–53), Mary I (1553–8), Elizabeth I (1558–1603), James I (and VI of Scotland) (1603–25), Charles I (1625–49), Charles II (1660–85) and James II (and VII of Scotland) (1685–88).

The poem can easily be found in full in a variety of versions, although it feels increasingly dated as some of the nicknames used are not familiar to modern

THE SIX WIVES OF HENRY VIII

One of the best known traditional mnemonics in British history recounts the fates of Henry VIII's six wives:

Divorced, beheaded, died,
Divorced, beheaded, survived.

If you have been studying his reign, you may well find that this is already enough to jog your memory as to the order of the wives, which is:

- Catherine of Aragon
  (mother of Mary I)
- Anne Boleyn
  (mother of Elizabeth I)
- Jane Seymour
  (mother of Edward VI)
- Anne of Cleves
- Catherine Howard
- Catherine Parr

Alternatively, there are two further traditional methods for recalling the wives. There is the couplet:

Kate and Anne and Jane,
And Anne and Kate again and again!

Or, to remember their surnames, you can use this mnemonic:

All Boys Should Come Home, Please.

readers. If you're hot on your history you may have noticed another small problem, which is that it has skipped the short but historically fascinating reign of Lady Jane Grey. Given the way that modern history is taught, you may find it more useful to learn shorter mnemonics for specific royal dynasties. For instance, the Tudors are a popular choice for study. The full list, including Lady Jane, is: Henry VII, Henry VIII, Edward VI, Lady Jane Grey (1553), Mary I (1553–8) and Elizabeth I (1558–1603). You could use this rhyme:

> Henry Seven, Henry Eight
> Edward Six and Lady Grey
> Bloody Mary, Elizabeth the First
> After Bloody Mary's Thirst

KEY DATES

Learning dates is a task that many people find difficult, especially when it comes to remembering them in exams. There are a few different strategies that can help with this. One option is to come up with a visual image that captures a connection with the event in question. For instance, for the Battle of Trafalgar (1805) you might think of an eighteen-year-old sailor at the battle holding up a hand with five outstretched fingers. There are also some nice rhymes that can be used, such as:

In fifteen hundred and eighty-eight
The Spanish Armada met its fate.

And for the date of the Gunpowder Plot:

In sixteen hundred and five
All in Parliament alive
Were hoped by rebels soon to die
By being blown into the sky.

An alternative approach to remembering dates is to use the method of letter counting: use a memorable phrase in which the number of letters in each word gives the digits of the year. For instance, for the Great Fire of London (1666), which started at a baker's house on Pudding Lane, we can use:

A London Bakery Burned.

The first word has 1 letter, the second 6, the third 6 and the fourth 6, giving us 1666. (If you happen to know Roman numerals, you can also remember this date by writing down one of each letter in descending order from 1000: MDCLXVI = 1000 + 500 + 100 + 50 + 10 + 5 + 1 = 1666.)

The Battle of Hastings (1066) presents us with a problem, which is that there are no words with zero letters. The solution is to use a ten-letter word instead. Imagine King Harold exclaiming this as he faces a hail of arrows:

I Capitulate, Cursed Arrows!

You can create your own mnemonics in this style, but here are a few more suggestions. For the Battle of Bosworth Field (1485), which ended the Wars of the Roses with a victory for the House of Lancaster over the House of York:

A Rosy Military Field.

For the English Bill of Rights, which left the monarch unable to raise taxes or an army without parliamentary consent (1689):

A Stuart Monarchy Unpowered.

For the Battle of Waterloo (1815):

I, Napoleon, A Loser?

For the end of the Second World War (1945):

A Firestorm Ends. Peace.

MEDIEVAL BATTLES

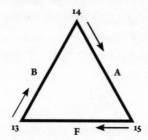

This is a visual mnemonic for the dates of three of the most significant medieval battles: Agincourt, Bannockburn and Flodden. You could remember the order of the battles with the mnemonic

Bring **A** **F**riend

then the diagram helps you remember the dates, thus:

- The Battle of **B**annockburn 1314
- The Battle of **A**gincourt 1415
- The Battle of **F**lodden 1513

SCOTLAND AND ENGLAND

Robert the Bruce's defeat of the English at Bannock-burn in 1314 preserved Scottish independence from England. So, when did Scotland and England finally join together? Well, it was a two-stage process: in 1603, James VI of Scotland took the throne as James I of England and declared the Union of the Crowns (of a joint realm which he called 'Britain'); then the Acts of Union were passed in England in 1706 and Scotland in 1707. This might help you remember the dates:

> The Crowns were joined in sixteen oh three
> By James the first and the sixth
> The Acts of Union, in the next century
> Were in seventeen oh seven and six.

THE GUNPOWDER PLOT

It's easy to forget how significant the struggle between Protestantism and Catholicism was in Britain's history. In the sixteenth and seventeenth centuries in particular, the religion of the monarch was hugely important, leading at various times to religious persecution for one or the other branch of Christianity.

In 1605 a group of Catholic aristocrats under the leadership of Robert Catesby planned to kill the Protestant James I at the state opening of parliament, using barrels of gunpowder as explosives. They aimed to replace him with his nine-year-old daughter Princess Elizabeth, who they would have treated as a puppet queen while bringing her up as a Catholic. The failure of the plot is still commemorated every year on Bonfire Night, when effigies of Guy Fawkes (who was caught on the scene) are burned. This rhyme records the story:

> Remember, remember the fifth of November,
> Gunpowder, treason and plot.
> We see no reason
> Why gunpowder treason
> Should ever be forgot!

Guy Fawkes, guy, 'twas his intent
To blow up king and parliament.
Three score barrels were laid below
To prove old England's overthrow.

By God's mercy he was catch'd
With a darkened lantern and burning match.
So, holler boys, holler boys, let the bells ring.
Holler boys, holler boys, God save the king.
And what shall we do with him?
Burn him!

BREAKTHROUGHS OF THE INDUSTRIAL REVOLUTION

This is a fairly unusual kind of mnemonic, which uses gestures, word resemblances and a story to drop hints about who invented which new process in the Industrial Revolution:

I had my friend **Eli with me**

We wanted to drink some **gin** [mime drinking]

We didn't have a clue **Watt** to do

Steam was coming out of our ears [gesture indicating ears]

So we drove to a **toll** booth

And dropped in some coins [mime dropping coins/
seeds]

Our grooves were playing on the radio

We were **spinning** around [pretend to be spinning]

On **our right** was the lake

With a steamboat passing by [mime **swimming**]

Our **best ever** day out ended up in a karaoke bar

With Eli and me **stealing** the show [dancing].

You could use this or your own variation on it to
remember: Eli Whitney's cotton gin; James Watt's
steam engine; Jethro Tull's seed drill; James
Hargreaves's spinning jenny; Richard Arkwright's
spinning frame; an advance in water power; and
Henry Bessemer's Bessemer method, an improve-
ment in steelmaking.

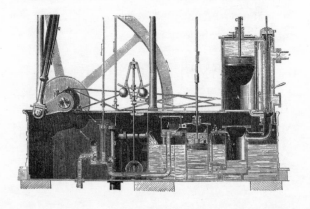

THE CAUSES OF THE FIRST WORLD WAR

History is rarely simple and it is overly simplistic to reduce the story of how the world wars started to a few words or events. For instance, we often read that the assassination of the Archduke Ferdinand in Sarajevo triggered the First World War but, to explain this, one would need a fairly detailed understanding of the impact the murder had on various diplomatic alliances and pacts. We can, however, at least offer the following mnemonic for remembering the **MAIN** causes of the war, in the hope it will remind students of the more complex underlying stories:

- **M**ilitarism
- **A**lliance System
- **I**mperialism
- **N**ationalism

BRITISH PRIME MINISTERS

To remember the British Prime Ministers since 1945, you could use this mnemonic:

> **A C**at **E**ats **M**y **D**ashing **W**hite **H**at. **W**hich **C**at?
> **T**hat's **M**y **B**lue **B**urmese **C**at, **M**an!

The Prime Ministers are: Clement **A**ttlee, Winston **C**hurchill, Anthony **E**den, Harold **M**acmillan, Alec **D**ouglas-Home, Harold **W**ilson, Edward **H**eath, Harold **W**ilson, James **C**allaghan, Margaret **T**hatcher, John **M**ajor, Tony **B**lair, Gordon **B**rown, David **C**ameron and Theresa **M**ay.

For the Prime Ministers from the First to the Second World War, you might need more than just a capital letter to remember the full list: Herbert Asquith, David Lloyd George, Andrew Bonar Law, Stanley Baldwin, James Ramsay MacDonald, Baldwin (again), MacDonald (again), Baldwin (again), Neville Chamberlain, Winston Churchill. You could create a miniature memory palace by visualizing this brief rhyme:

> A quiff, Georgie Porgy, a rag and bone man,
> Baldy, Maccy D, again, again, again.
> Chamberlain claimed it's 'peace in our time'.
> Then Churchill came in and finished the rhyme.

Alternatively, you could use a shorter mnemonic such as:

> **A G**ood-Looking **B**aker **M**utters **B**ut **M**akes **B**rilliant **C**ream **C**akes.

(If they are more to your taste, you can swap custard creams for the cream cakes.)

ONCE I CAUGHT A FISH ALIVE

———◆———

Number Tricks and Easy Maths

The world of maths and numbers is essentially an abstract realm: as a result, mnemonics and visualizations can be tremendously useful to getting information, formulas and ideas to stick in your head. In this chapter, we will look at easy ways to remember a variety of numerical and mathematical facts.

FINGER COUNTING

One reason why the decimal system of numbering has been so popular over the millennia is that we have a ready-made mnemonic for the numbers from one to ten (our fingers) and even from eleven to twenty (our toes).

Here's a rhyme which can be accompanied by a 'countdown' on your fingers if you are telling it to a child …

Ten fat sausages, sizzling in a pan,
one went pop and one went bang!
Eight fat sausages, sizzling in a pan,
one went pop and one went bang!
Six fat sausages, sizzling in a pan,
one went pop and one went bang!
Four fat sausages, sizzling in a pan,
one went pop and one went bang!
Two fat sausages, sizzling in a pan,
one went pop and one went bang!
No fat sausages sizzling in a pan.

In a similar vein, this is the first verse of a classic bathtime rhyme:

Five little ducks went swimming one day.
Over the hills and far away.
Mother Duck said 'Quack Quack Quack Quack!'
But only four little ducks came back!

(I'll assume you can work out the remaining verses for yourself … You can finish with 'zero little ducks came back' or 'no little ducks came back'.)

COUNTING RHYMES

From ten green bottles on a wall to a partridge in a pear tree and from 'Hickory Dickory Dock' to those ants that come marching one by one, there is a huge range of other songs and rhymes that rely on counting. Often, this is also the first way we teach children about numbers. For instance, the rhyme 'Once I Caught a Fish Alive' is a classic that has been used in nurseries around the world over the centuries.

> One, two, three, four, five,
> Once I caught a fish alive.
> Six, seven, eight, nine, ten,
> Then I let him go again.
> Why did you let him go?
> Because he bit my finger so.
> Which finger did he bite?
> This little finger on my right!

Here is another well-known classic:

One, two, buckle my shoe,
Three, four, knock at the door,
Five, six, pick up sticks,
Seven, eight, lay them straight,
Nine, ten, a big fat hen,
Eleven, twelve, dig and delve,
Thirteen, fourteen, maids a-courting,
Fifteen, sixteen, maids in the kitchen,
Seventeen, eighteen, maids in waiting,
Nineteen, twenty, my plate's empty.

WRITING NUMBERS

Some nursery teachers also use rhymes to teach children the shapes of numbers (these can be used with visual images of the 'route' your pencil should take in forming the numerals):

Around and around and around we go,
    when we get home we have a zero
Number one is like a stick,
    a straight line that is also quick
Around and back on the railroad track,
    two, two, two, two
Around a tree, around a tree,
    that's the way to make a three

Down and over, down once more,
    that's the way to make a four
Straight line down, then around,
    hat on top and five's a clown
Make a curve then make a loop,
    number six rolls a hoop
Across the sky and down from heaven,
    that's how you make a seven
Make an 'S' and do not wait,
    go back up and that's an eight
A loop and a line, that makes a nine
Straight line down, then around with a grin,
    that's the way to make a ten!

Alternatively, you could try teaching the numbers with a simpler visual reference, which can be adapted into flashcards or drawings:

0 resembles a ball or the sun.
1 resembles a pencil or a pen.
2 resembles a swan.
3 resembles an ear, or the lips on your face.
4 resembles a yacht.
5 resembles a snake or a key.
6 resembles a comet or a yo-yo.
7 resembles a flag or a knee.
8 resembles a snowman or an hourglass.
9 resembles a balloon on a string.

THE MNEMONIC MAJOR SYSTEM

For a more advanced use of numbers in memory tasks, the major system (also known as the phonetic number system or Herigone's mnemonic system) is a technique for memorizing numbers by converting them into consonants, then into words. It is widely used by magicians as a way of startling audiences with their powers of recall.

There are variations on the system, but here is one of the most basic:

For 0, substitute an 's' (because the start of 'zero' sounds like an 's' and 's' is more use in forming words than 'z').

For 1 substitute a 't' (because 't' has one downstroke).

For 2 substitute an 'n' (because 'n' has two downstrokes).

For 3 substitute an 'm' (because 'm' has three downstrokes).

For 4 substitute a 'r' (because 'four' ends in 'r').

For 5 substitute a 'l' (because L is the Roman numeral for fifty).

For 6 substitute a 'j' or a 'g' (because 'g' is a 6 upside down, and 'g' and 'j' can have a similar sound).

For 7 substitute a 'k' or 'c' (because 'k' can be formed from two sevens).

For 8 substitute a 'f' or 'v' (because a handwritten 'f' can look like an 8).

For 9 substitute a 'p' or 'b' (as they are both reflections of the numeral '9').

If we want to memorize the number 43394, we can now convert it into the letters 'rmmbr'. Then by adding in vowels we can make the word 'remember', so this word can be used as a memory cue for the number.

Or for 3.14159 (the number pi to five decimal places) you could convert to mtrtlp then add vowels to form the words 'meter tulip', and think of a metre-long ruler with a tulip on it to remember the numerals.

THE PEG SYSTEM

A related approach comes from the 'peg' system, which is often used by memory grand masters (in other words, people who compete in memory competitions). This involves assigning an object to each number and then forming visual associations – in this respect, it is a similar method to the memory palace we discussed in the introduction.

One version of this method uses rhyming pegs for the numbers from one to ten, as below:

One = bun
Two = shoe
Three = tree
Four = door
Five = hive
Six = bricks
Seven = heaven
Eight = weight
Nine = wine
Ten = hen

The peg system can be used to memorize numbers, but it is possibly most effective when it comes to lists: in order to remember four items of shopping, for instance cheese, wrapping paper, sausages and a tin of beans, you would picture a cheese bun, a shoe wrapped up in paper, some sausages hanging in a tree, and a tin of beans balanced on a door.

Another adaptation of the system is the person–action–object system in which each number is associated with one of each class. (For instance, the number 37 might correspond to Leonardo DiCaprio buying a fish, number 23 might correspond to Edith Piaf smashing a champagne glass, while number 97 might correspond to King Arthur holding the holy grail. Then, to remember the sequence 37-23-97 the person using this peg system would picture Leonardo DiCaprio smashing the holy grail.)

Some memory grand masters use versions of the peg system that go up to a hundred or even a thousand places, although for most mere mortals it is best used in a more basic way.

BODMAS, BIDMAS OR PEMDAS?

When it comes to mathematics, and arithmetic in particular, one of the best-known mnemonics is BODMAS. This is a reminder of the order in which you should carry out operations when working out a sum.

You might want to use a sentence such as

Bring **O**nly **D**ead **M**en **A**fter **S**ix

to remember this, but it's probably easier to just remember the word itself. It stands for **B**rackets. **O**rders, **D**ivision, **M**ultiplication, **A**ddition, **S**ubtraction.

Before expanding on this, it's worth noting that there are variations on this acronym – some people prefer to remember 'orders' as 'indices' so learn BIDMAS instead. And in the United States, the standard mnemonic is PEMDAS, which stands for **P**arentheses, **E**xponents, **M**ultiplication, **D**ivision, **A**ddition, **S**ubtraction. Parentheses are the same as brackets and exponents are the same as indices (which indicate orders).

To remember PEMDAS you can use

Please **E**xcuse **M**y **D**ear **A**unt **S**ally.

Whichever mnemonic you use, the next question is: what does it all mean?

Let's say we are confronted with an equation such as this:

$$3^2 - 5 \div (8 - 3) \times 2 + 6$$

The steps we take in applying the BODMAS rule are:

- ⤳ STEP 1: First perform any calculations inside brackets and simplify orders.

- ⤳ STEP 2: Perform all multiplications and divisions, working from left to right.

- ⤳ STEP 3: Perform all additions and subtractions, working from left to right.

You may have spotted that PEMDAS and BODMAS place multiplication and division in a different order. The reason this doesn't matter is that in Step 2 we give the two operations the same status, just as we do for addition and subtraction in the final step, simply working from left to right.

So, first we should deal with the brackets and the orders. Orders are numbers such as 3^2 (which is three squared): the indices or exponents are the superscript numbers that indicate what order of a number we are dealing with (whether it is squared, cubed, a square root or whatever).

For Step 1, we can simplify the equation thus:

$$3^2 - 5 \div (8 - 3) \times 2 + 6$$
$$9 - 5 \div 5 \times 2 + 6$$

For Step 2 we can deal with the multiplication and division:

$$9 - 5 \div 5 \times 2 + 6$$
$$9 - 1 \times 2 + 6$$
$$9 - 2 + 6$$

And for the last step we work through the additions and subtractions:

$$9 - 2 + 6$$
$$7 + 6$$
$$13$$

So whether you BODMAS, BIDMAS or PEMDAS, you will reach the same answer, and hopefully the correct one.

LONG DIVISION

Long division seems to be a dying art now that calculators and other mobile devices are used so widely. It may be a skill that you need, however, whether for exams or in case your phone or computer loses power, so here's a way to remember the stages of the process.

The order in which you need to do things is **D**ivide, **M**ultiply, **S**ubtract, **B**ring down, which you can remember with the mnemonic:

Dead **M**onkeys **S**mell **B**ad,

To explain how this works, you write down a sum such as 3723 / 17 thus:

$$17\overline{\smash{)}3723}$$

First, you look at 3723, from left to right, for a number big enough for us to be able to **divide** by 17; 3 isn't big enough, but 37 is 2 × 17 (with a remainder of 3). So, we write 2 above the 7, then **multiply** this by 17 to get 34. We write this under the 37 and **subtract** it from 37 to get 3. Then we **bring down** the next number, 2, giving us 32.

Again, we can **divide** this by 17, giving us 1 (with a remainder of 15). We write 1 above the 2, **multiply** 17 by 1, **subtract** from 32 to get 15 and **bring down** the final digit 3, giving us 153.

Finally, we **divide** this by 17 to give us 9 with no remainder: we write the 9 on top above the last 3, and we have the answer 219.

$$
\begin{array}{r}
219 \\
17\overline{\smash{)}3723} \\
34 \\
32 \\
17 \\
153
\end{array}
$$

Depending on how you learned arithmetic, other methods of division may seem more intuitive, but when it comes to much larger numbers this can be the best way to keep track of the process.

FRACTIONS

When you use fractions such as ¾, it's easy to get the numerator and denominator mixed up. (In this case, 3 is the numerator and 4 is the denominator, meaning that the fraction represents 3 units, each of a quarter, in other words three-quarters.)

The best way to remember which is which is to use the simple mnemonic

NUmerator **U**p, **D**enominator **D**own.

MEAN, MEDIAN, MODE

If you get stuck when you try to remember the different kinds of 'average' that are used in statistics, here is a useful variation on the traditional nursery rhyme that will help you to pin down the differences:

Hey diddle diddle,
The **median**'s the middle,

You add then divide for the **mean**,
The **mode** is the one that is there the most,
The **range** is the difference between.

So, given this ordered list of values, 3, 4, 4, 4, 5, 6, 6, 8, 14, we can say that the median is 5 (the value in the middle of the list), the mean is the total (54) divided by the number of values (9), which is 6, and the mode is 4 (which appears most often in the list). The range is 11 (the difference between 3 and 14).

MULTIPLYING OUT FACTORS

Before you are taught how to find the factors of a quadratic equation you will often be asked to get used to the reverse process of multiplying factors together. For instance, you need to know how to multiply:

There are two good ways to remember this. The first is to remember **FOIL**. This means you multiply together the two terms in the first place (a × a). Then you multiply the two **o**uter numbers (a × b), the two **i**nner numbers (b × a) and the two numbers in the last place (b × b). Then you add these together to get $a^2 + ab + ba + b^2$. ab is the same as ba so we can simplify this as $a^2 + 2ab + b^2$.

Alternatively, you might find it easier to remember 'the man with a big nose' as depicted in this image:

$$(x - 3)(x + 5)$$

ROMAN NUMERALS AND THE METRIC SYSTEM

Before the decimal numbering system came into use, Roman numerals were one of the various systems around the world used to record numbers. Historically, they have been used to date buildings, books and monuments, among other things. The system uses the following letters to represent numbers:

- I = 1
- V = 5
- X = 10
- L = 50
- C = 100
- D = 500
- M = 1,000

Numbers are written from left to right, for instance LXXI represents 50 + 10 + 10 + 1 = 71. It is important to remember that a smaller value placed to the left of a larger value should be subtracted, for instance XI represents 11 while IX represents 9.

The traditional mnemonic for this sequence is

I Value **X**ylophones **L**ike **C**ows **D**ig **M**ilk.

In the metric system of measurements, the challenge is to remember the prefixes that tell us that, for instance, a kilogram is 1,000 grams, while a centimetre is a hundredth of a metre.

Going from a thousand times the base unit down to a thousandth of the base unit, the prefixes are as follows: Kilo-, Hecto-, Deca-, (Base), Deci-, Centi-, Milli-.

You can use one of the following mnemonics for this sequence:

Kittens **H**ate **D**ogs, **B**ut **D**o **C**hase **M**ice.

or

Kings **H**ate **D**ragons **B**ecause **D**ragons **C**an't **M**ove.

TRIGONOMETRY

Trigonometry is not as scary as it might sound. If you have a right-angled triangle, all you need to know is the length of two of the sides, or the length of one side and an angle, in order to be able to work out the length of the other sides or angles.

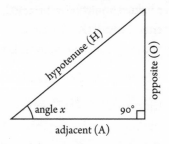

adjacent (A)

For instance, in this triangle, consider the angle marked *x*. The opposite side is marked O, the adjacent side is marked A, and the hypotenuse is the side opposite the right angle. The equations you need to know are:

> The **S**ine of the angle = the ratio of the **O**pposite side to the **H**ypotenuse
>
> The **C**osine of the angle = the ratio of the **A**djacent side to the **H**ypotenuse
>
> The **T**angent of the angle = the ratio of the **O**pposite and the **A**djacent sides

If you know, for instance, the length of the hypotenuse is 10cm and the angle is 30 degrees, then to find out the length of the adjacent side you write down sin 30 = A/10 and then work through this equation to find A.

The initials of the equations above spell out **SOH–CAH–TOA**, which, as it has the sound of a Hawaiian volcano or tribal chief, most people find easy to remember. You could also resort to a variety of mnemonics, including:

Some **O**ld **H**airy **C**amels **A**re **H**airier **T**han **O**thers **A**re.

Some **O**f **H**er **C**hildren **A**re **H**aving **T**rouble **O**ver **A**lgebra.

She **O**ffered **H**er **C**at **A** **H**eavy **T**easpoon **O**f **A**cid.

Or for the reverse order **TOA-CAH-SOH**:

Two **O**ld **A**ngels **C**arrying **A**ncient **H**arps **S**kipped **O**ver **H**eaven.

A SLICE OF PI

When calculating the area or circumference of a circle, you need to remember the two formulas below:

$$\text{Circumference} = \text{pi} \times \text{diameter} = \pi d$$
$$\text{Area} = \text{pi} \times \text{radius squared} = \pi r^2$$

(Circumference is the length around the edge of a circle, diameter is the width at the widest point, and radius is half of the diameter, which is the distance from the centre of the circle to the edge.)

PYTHAGORAS'S THEOREM

The other traditional way of calculating the length of one of the sides of a right-angled triangle comes from Pythagoras's Theorem, which states simply that the square of the hypotenuse is equal to the sum of the squares on the other two sides. There is a long, mnemonic tall tale for remembering this, which involves describing three Native American 'squaws' who are each sitting on different animal hides. Of course, it turns out that squaw on the hippopotamus (who has two children) is equal to the sum of the squaws on the other two sides (who have one child each).

I'm uncomfortable with recounting the full story, because of the casual use of the archaic term 'squaws' (which has also been used in a derogatory way over the years). And that's not to mention the more pedantic objection of how unlikely it would be for her to be sitting on a hippo hide in the first place, given that hippos aren't found in the Americas.

Perhaps it would be simpler to picture a square painted on the side of a hippopotamus that is equal to the sum of the squares painted on the sides on two other animals (let's say a lion and a rhinoceros) as they drink water together at the river.

Or, if you'd rather not meditate on African wildlife, just remember the image below, and the fact that one of the squares is the same size as the other two put together: it should be pretty obvious that the square on the hypotenuse is the biggest one.

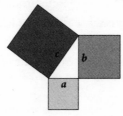

There's a short mnemonic that can help you to remember which is which:

Cherry pie is delicious.
Apple pies are too!

To explain: think of this rhyme:

Cherry (**C**) pie (**π**) is delicious (**d**)
Apple (**A**) pies (**π**) are (**r**) too (**²**).

Sometimes you see this mnemonic with the first line reading 'Cherry **pies are** delicious', but it's best to stick to the version above to avoid getting confused about which iteration of 'are' is supposed to indicate the **r**adius.

SOME TRICKY NUMBERS TO REMEMBER

Finally, here are a few mnemonics for important numbers, in which the number of letters in each word represents a digit in the decimal expansion: pi to six decimal places (3.141592):

How I wish I could calculate pi.

pi to twenty decimal places (3.141592653589793 23846):

Now, I wish I could recollect pi. 'Eureka,' cried the
great inventor. Christmas pudding, Christmas pie,
is the problem's very centre.

The square root of 2 to three decimal places (1,414):

I wish I knew (the square root of two).

The square root of 3 to three decimal places (1.732):

O, charmed was he (to know the root of three).

e to five decimal places (also known as Euler's
number, the base of the natural logarithms – 2.71828):

In realism, I advocate my mnemonic.

phi to six decimal places (the golden ratio: 1.618034):

A golden, a rational mathematic too pure.

(Note that 'mathematic', with ten letters, represents
the zero.)

THIRTY DAYS HATH SEPTEMBER

───❖───

Calendars, Geography and Maps

In this chapter we will be looking at planet Earth: this includes ways to remember how the planetary cycles are recorded in calendars, how to read the phases of the moon, and a variety of aspects of the geography of our world.

THE MONTHS OF THE YEAR

Since prehistory, humankind has been fascinated by the planetary cycles: the rotation of the Earth creates the cycle of day and night, the lunar cycle gives us new moons and full moons, while the solar year regulates the seasons. These cycles are the basis of all calendars. They do not fit perfectly together, however: 12 lunar months take approximately 354 days and 8 hours, whereas the solar year lasts for about 365 days and 5 hours. This is the fundamental reason why we can't use a regular calendar of twelve thirty-day months, and why we need leap years. In addition, our current months derive from the Roman calendar, in which certain months were given extra emphasis for political reasons. So our calendar is a bit messy, and inevitably so. Luckily there is a well-known rhyme that addresses this problem.

The earliest known version of the rhyme is actually in Latin, from a 1488 book of verse:

Junius Aprilis September et ipse November
Dant triginta dies reliquis supadditur unus,
De quorum numero Februarius excipiatur.

Which translates as:

June, April, September, and November itself
Give thirty days, the rest add one more,
From which number February is excepted.

A more modern version is:

Thirty days hath September,
April, June, and November;
All the rest have thirty-one,
Excepting February alone,
And that has twenty-eight days clear,
And twenty-nine in each leap year.

(There are different versions: the first two lines, being the most memorable, tend to stay the same, while the fiddlier bit about February varies.)

KNUCKLE MONTHS

Another way to remember the months that have thirty-one days is to clench both your fists with the knuckles upwards and count from left to right, using both the knuckles (of which there are four, excluding the thumb) and the spaces between them. On your left hand, the little finger knuckle is January, the space is February, the fourth finger knuckle is March and so on up to July on the index finger knuckle. On your right hand, the index finger knuckle is August, the space is September and you get to December on the fourth finger knuckle (you don't need the little finger on the right hand).

So, the knuckles are January, March, May, July, August, October and December. And these are all the months that have thirty-one days. The spaces are February (which you should remember is the oddity with only twenty-eight or twenty-nine days), then April, June, September and November, which have only thirty days.

PHASES OF THE MOON

Another aspect of the lunar cycle that you may wish to remember is the way in which the moon changes from new moon to full and back again. In the northern hemisphere, the waxing moon (which is on the way from new moon to full) has a curve similar to that in 'D' while the waning moon is curved similar to a 'C'. So, it is traditional to remember the letters 'DOC' to represent the waxing, full and waning moon. An old saying that also captures this cycle is

Dog comes in the room, **C**at goes out.

There are some interesting variations on this in different languages. In those that derive from Latin, it can often be said that the moon is a liar since is resembles a 'C' (for *crescere* meaning 'to grow' in Latin) when it is waning and a D (for *decrescere* meaning to decrease) when it is waxing. On the contrary, Russians have a bit more trust in the moon's veracity, since the waxing moon takes the curve of the letter 'P' (for *растущая* or 'growing') and the waning moon the letter 'C' (for *стареющая* or 'getting old').

Going back to the English language, you might prefer to picture the curves in a lower case 'b' and 'd', in which case the **b**aby moon is waxing, and the **d**ying moon is waning.

Remember that if you are in the southern hemisphere, the process is the other way around, in which case you simply need to think of a COD swimming in the ocean or a wax candle. If by any chance you are directly on the equator, it is quite disconcerting to see the waxing or waning moon, as both are crescents lit from below by the sun, so mnemonics are no use to you when it comes to telling the two apart. On the bright side, this means that moon will never frown at you at the equator: it only knows how to smile!

MONTHS OF THE YEAR

If you need a quick way to remember the order of the months of the year you could use the mnemonic

> Just For Me, A Mouse Jumps Jelly, And Somebody Orange Never Diets.

Or a pithier version is

> Just For MAM, Jammy JASON Dances.

The traditional Victorian poem below provides a more longwinded way of recording the order (and typical weather) of the months.

> January brings the snow that
> Makes our feet and fingers glow.

February brings the rain that
Thaws the frozen lake again.
March brings breezes sharp and shrill that
Shake the dancing daffodil.
April brings the primrose sweet and
Scatters daisies at our feet.
May brings flocks of pretty lambs,
Skipping by their fleecy dams.
June brings tulips, lilies, and roses that
Fill the children's hands with posies.
Hot July brings cooling showers,
Apricots and gillyflowers.
August brings the sheaves of corn and
Then the harvest home is borne.
Warm September brings the fruit;
Sportsmen then begin to shoot.
Brown October brings the pheasant;
Then to gather nuts is pleasant.
Dull November brings the blast;
Then the leaves go whirling past.
Chill December brings the sleet,
Blazing fire and Christmas treat.

There is an amusing alternative version of this rhyme
by Flanders and Swann, which takes a gloomier
approach, ending up with:

Dark November brings the fog
Should not do it to a dog,

Freezing wet December then:
Bloody January again!

THE ZODIAC AND THE CHINESE CALENDAR

In China, each year is named after an animal, and there is a repeating cycle of twelve years: Rat, Bull, Tiger, Rabbit, Dragon, Snake, Horse, Goat, Monkey, Rooster, Dog, Boar. You could use this mnemonic to memorize the cycle:

Rice **B**iscuits **T**aste **R**adical

Dipping **S**auce **H**as **G**luten

More **R**ice, **D**rop and **B**oil.

In 2000 it was the year of the Dragon so, to calculate the current year, count around the cycle from there.

With the Western astrological zodiac, there is also a partial animal theme (mixed with some ancient mythology). The astrological months are as below.

- **A**ries (the Ram) starts on 21 March
- **T**aurus (the Bull) 21 April
- **G**emini (the Twins) 21 May
- **C**ancer (the Crab) 21 June
- **L**eo (the Lion) 21 July
- **V**irgo (the Virgin) 23 August
- **L**ibra (the Scales) 23 September
- **S**corpio (the Scorpio) 23 October
- **S**agittarius (the Archer) 23 November
- **C**apricorn (the Goat) 23 December
- **A**quarius (the Water-bearer) 21 January
- **P**isces (the Fishes) 20 February

Here are a couple of alternative mnemonics for remembering the order: I like the first one as it refers to the constellations, although the second may be more memorable.

All **T**he **G**reat **C**onstellations **L**ive **V**ery **L**ong **S**ince **S**tars **C**an't **A**lter **P**hysics.

A **T**ense **G**rey **C**at **L**ay **V**ery **L**ow **S**neaking **S**lowly, **C**ontemplating **A** **P**ounce.

DAYLIGHT SAVING

The fiddly business of changing the clocks in spring and autumn is quite a recent invention, having been first proposed in the late nineteenth century and adopted in the German Empire and Austria-Hungary during the First World War in 1916. (It is often wrongly suggested that it was invented by Benjamin Franklin, who notably claimed that 'early to bed and early to rise makes a man healthy, wealthy and wise'. This is not quite accurate, however, since his suggestion was merely that one should limit the use of artificial light such as candles in order to force people to make better use of the daylight hours.)

If you are familiar with American English rather than British English, the easiest way to remember which direction the clocks change in is the mnemonic:

Spring forwards, Fall back.

And for British readers who are suspicious of Americanisms, it is worth noting that the use of 'fall' instead of 'autumn' actually originated in England, being used for instance by Elizabeth I's tutor Roger Ascham in an archery manual, where the seasons are listed as 'Spring tyme, Somer, faule of the leafe, and winter'.

GEOGRAPHY

As well as understanding the pattern of the rotation of planet Earth, you may want to learn more about the geography of the planet. And one place to start in that quest would be making sure you at least know how to spell geography:

> **G**eorge's **E**lderly **O**ld **G**randfather **R**ode **A** **P**ig **H**ome **Y**esterday.

THE POINTS OF THE COMPASS

The standard mnemonic for the points of the compass, North, East, South and West, is, of course:

> **N**ever **E**at **S**hredded **W**heat.

As with other old standards, there are lots of alternative versions, including:

Naughty **E**lephants **S**pray **W**ater.

Never **E**at **S**limy **W**orms.
Never **E**ver **S**moke **W**eed.
Never **E**at **S**oggy **W**afers.

One of my favourite stories on the subject comes from Lord Brocket who, having been imprisoned on attempted fraud charges, found himself teaching some of his less-educated fellow prisoners some general knowledge, including how to read a map. When he realized one of them didn't know which directions were 'up' and 'down' on a map he taught him to remember 'N' for 'nut' (slang for head) and 'S' for 'shoe'.

RINGS AROUND THE WORLD

When looking at a globe of the world, as well as an understanding of the points of the compass, it is useful to understand latitude, longitude and the tropics. To distinguish latitude and longitude, it may be best to remember the etymology of the words – 'latitude' is related to 'lateral', meaning 'sideways', while 'longitude' is related to length. The longitude lines are all the same length and run through the poles (as opposed to the latitude lines which are different lengths and all run parallel to the equator).

Alternatively, you might find it easier to remember that 'lat lays flat', meaning that the latitude lines are flat horizontally when you look at a globe with the north pole at the top.

For the tropics, which are lines of latitude that are north and south of the equator, here is a mnemonic that packs in a lot of information:

Ca-**n**-cer = **2** letters + (n halfway = ½°N) + **3** letters = **23½°N**

Capric-**o**-rn (which is **o**pposite) is **23½°S**.

Alternatively, you could just remember that:

Ca**N**cer is **N**orth and Capric**O**rn is **O**pposite.

The importance of the tropics lies in the fact that the sun is directly overhead at the Tropic of Cancer on 21 June (the summer solstice in the northern hemisphere) and is at the Tropic of Capricorn on 21 December (the winter solstice in the northern hemisphere and vice versa).

LAND AND SEA

Here are a few more mnemonics that can help you to remember geographical features of the world.

The five oceans of the world, in descending order of size are: Pacific, Atlantic, Indian, Southern and Arctic. You could remember this using one of these phrases:

Pigs **A**ttack **I**n **S**trange **A**ttire.

Polish **A**rmy **I**n **S**udden **A**ttack.

For the six different types of land terrain – tundra, deciduous forests, deserts, grasslands, tropical rainforests and coniferous forests – you could remember:

The **D**ry **D**esert **G**ets **T**remendously **C**old.

For the seven continents, Europe, Asia, Africa, Australia, Antarctica, North America and South America:

Eat **A**n **A**pple **A**s **A** **N**ice **S**nack.

Here's a list of the longest rivers in the world in descending order of length. Note that it is difficult to find two academics who agree on how to measure river lengths, so this is only one version of the many possible variations on the list:

- Nile (Africa), 4145 miles

- Amazon (S. America), 4050 miles

- Mississippi-Missouri (USA), 3760 miles

- Irtysh (Russia), 3200 miles

- Yangtse (China), 3100 miles

- Amur (Asia), 2900 miles

- Congo (Africa), 2718 miles

- Huang-Ho (or Yellow) (China), 2700 miles

Newts And Moles In Your Amazing Country House.

For the Great Lakes of North America, which are, from west to east, Lake Superior, Lake Michigan, Lake Huron, Lake Erie and Lake Ontario, you could use **HOMES** if you just want to remember the five names. For the correct order, you can use:

Sally Made Henry Eat Onions.

Or starting from the east:

Old Elephants Have Much Skin.

You can also use the brand name Lenor for remembering where the Niagara Falls are on a map:

Left – **E**rie – **N**iagara – **O**ntario – **R**ight.

THE WEATHER

If you have ever got the spellings of 'whether' and 'weather' mixed up, you can remember the correct way using the following phrases:

Whether it is here, or whether it is there, whether is not quite where nor there.

Heather likes the **weather** hot.

(And if you aren't certain of the spelling of heather, remember it grows on a heath.)

One of the best-known rhymes about the weather is a reminder of what is likely to ensue when the sky is red:

Red sky at night: shepherd's delight.
Red sky in the morning: shepherd's warning.
Red sky in the morning: travellers take warning.
Red sky at night: travellers' delight.

(In some versions 'Red sky' is replaced by 'Rainbow' in the third and fourth line of this rhyme, and 'shepherd' is often replaced by 'sailor' since both were professions in the past where the ability to predict the weather was crucial.)

A pithier related rhyme is:

Evening red and morning grey,
Two sure signs of one fine day.

Another traditional weather rhyme that can still be extremely accurate is:

Mackerel sky, mackerel sky,
Never long wet, never long dry.

(A 'mackerel sky' is one where the cloud pattern resembles the scales on a fish.)

And this rhyme is a reminder of how air pressure tends to translate into weather conditions:

High to Low,
Look Out Below;
Low to High,
Clear Blue Sky!

Finally, this is more of a parody of the 'red sky' rhyme: some Scouts have been taught to remember that the fundamental rule of camping is:

Dark sky at night, you're up too late,
Dark sky in the morning, you are up too early.

THE COLOURS
OF THE RAINBOW

We traditionally learn that there are seven colours in the rainbow: red, orange, yellow, green, blue, indigo and violet. The distinctions between blue, indigo and violet are controversial: the inclusion of indigo seems to date to Isaac Newton who, as well as being a great scientist, was prone to superstition and was fascinated by alchemy. The story is that he imposed a seventh colour because of the magical or sacred properties of the number seven. We shouldn't be too pedantic, however, as we could equally argue that, as a continuum, the rainbow could be arbitrarily divided into any number of colours. So, let's stick with the traditional version of seven colours.

Some people simply remember that **Roy G. Biv** sounds like a person's name (or even a planet or asteroid). Alternatively, the most commonly used mnemonic historically has been:

Richard **O**f **Y**ork **G**ave **B**attle **I**n **V**ain.

Or you might prefer a more religious version:

Read **O**ut **Y**our **G**ood **B**ook **I**n **V**erse.

A CAT HAS CLAWS AT THE ENDS OF ITS PAWS

Grammar and Language

Rules about grammar, language and writing are not set in stone – what is seen as normal changes over time: Chaucer's works are virtually incomprehensible to modern readers; the semicolon was invented only in the fifteenth century (by a Venetian printer); and, in the sixteenth century, a double negative wasn't regarded as bad grammar. Even writing from a hundred years ago can seem quite stilted and odd to us today.

How grammar and language will mutate over time under the influence of the internet and social media remains to be seen. Either way, there are some rules and principles that you do need to know: this chapter introduces some of the mnemonics that may help you to write better English, as well as looking at some of the quirks of the language, and how we learn it in the first place.

A IS FOR APPLE PIE

Of course any language starts with an alphabet, and one of the first things many children learn in schools is the alphabet song, which takes the same tune as 'Twinkle, Twinkle, Little Star' or 'Baa, Baa, Black Sheep'.

A-B-C-D-E-F-G
H-I-J-K-LMNOP
Q-R-S
T-U-V
W and X
Y and Zee
Now I know my 'ABCs'
Next time won't you sing with me?

Or, if you prefer the British 'zed' sound for the letter 'z' rather than the American 'zee', you can finish it thus

Sugar on your bread
Eat it all up before you are dead.

There are also many variations on the 'Apple Pie' nursery rhyme, which traditionally starts 'A was for apple pie, B bit it, C cut it ...' For instance, here is a nineteenth-century variation:

Says A, give me a good large slice,
Says B, a little bit, but nice,
Says C, cut me a piece of crust,
Take it, says D, it's dry as dust,
Says E, I'll eat it fast, I will,
Says F, I vow I'll have my fill,
Says G, give it me good and great,
Says H, a little bit I hate,
Says I, it's ice I must request,
Says J, the juice I love the best,
Says K, let's keep it up above,
Says L, the border's what I love,
Says M, it makes your teeth to chatter,
N said, it's nice, there's naught the matter,
O others' plates with grief surveyed,
P for a large piece begged and prayed,
Q quarrelled for the topmost slice,
R rubbed his hands and said, 'It's nice,'
S silent sat, and simply looked,
T thought, and said, it's nicely cooked,
U understood the fruit was cherry,
V vanished when they all got merry,
W wished there'd been a quince in,
X here explained he'd need convincing,
Y said, I'll eat, and yield to none,
Z, like a zany, said he'd done,
While ampersand purloined the dish,
And for another pie did wish.

Edward Lear once parodied this with a poem that started 'A was once an apple pie / Pidy / Widy / Tidy / Pidy / Nice insidy / Apple pie.' But his 'Nonsense Alphabet' is possibly more fun:

A was an ant, Who seldom stood still,
And who made a nice house, In the side of a hill.
B was a book, With a binding of blue,
And pictures and stories, For me and for you.
C was a cat, Who ran after a rat;
But his courage did fail, When she seized on his tail.
D was a duck, With spots on his back,
Who lived in the water, And always said 'Quack!'
E was an elephant, Stately and wise:
He had tusks and a trunk, And two queer little eyes.
F was a fish, Who was caught in a net;
But he got out again, And is quite alive yet.
G was a goat, Who was spotted with brown:
When he did not lie still, He walked up and down.
H was a hat, Which was all on one side;
Its crown was too high, And its brim was too wide.
I was some ice, So white and so nice,
But which nobody tasted, And so it was wasted.
J was a jackdaw, Who hopped up and down
In the principal street, Of a neighbouring town.
K was a kite, Which flew out of sight,
Above houses so high, Quite into the sky.
L was a light, Which burned all the night,
And lighted the gloom, Of a very dark room.

M was a mill, Which stood on a hill,
And turned round and round,
With a loud hummy sound.
N was a net, Which was thrown in the sea
To catch fish for dinner, For you and for me.
O was an orange, So yellow and round:
When it fell off the tree, It fell down to the ground.
P was a pig, Who was not very big;
But his tail was too curly, And that made him surly.
Q was a quail, With a very short tail;
And he fed upon corn, In the evening and morn.
R was a rabbit, Who had a bad habit
Of eating the flowers, In gardens and bowers.
S was the sugar-tongs, Sippity-see,
To take up the sugar, To put in our tea.
T was a tortoise, All yellow and black:
He walked slowly away, And he never came back.
U was an urn, All polished and bright,
And full of hot water, At noon and at night.
V was a villa, Which stood on a hill,
By the side of a river, And close to a mill.
W was a whale, With a very long tail,
Whose movements were frantic, Across the Atlantic.
X was King Xerxes, Who, more than all Turks, is
Renowned for his fashion, Of fury and passion.
Y was a yew, Which flourished and grew
By a quiet abode, Near the side of a road.
Z was some zinc, So shiny and bright,
Which caused you to wink, In the sun's merry light.

PANGRAMS

A pangram is a sentence that uses all of the letters in the alphabet. The best-known English example is:

The quick brown fox jumps over the lazy dog.

This contains thirty-five letters: there are several shorter versions including these twenty-eight-letter ones:

Jived fox nymph grabs quick waltz.

Glib jocks quiz nymph to vex dwarf.

A perfect pangram is one with each of the twenty-six letters of the alphabet used only once. The sentence below achieves this but is regarded as a bit of a cheat as it uses abbreviations:

Mr Jock, TV quiz PhD, bags few lynx.

VOWELS AND PHONEMES

If you need to remember the five vowels in the alphabet, think of the following sentence:

Angry **E**lephant **I**n **O**range **U**nderpants.

The letter 'y' isn't included above. It is a bit of a double agent in the world of letters: it is also known as a semi-vowel as it functions as a vowel in a world such as 'fly' but as a consonant in 'yellow'.

Linguists know that there aren't just the five vowels in the English language. For a start, they list fourteen 'monophthongs' and 'narrow diphthongs', which are expressed in notation as uː, ʊ, əʊ, ɔː, ɒ, ɑː, ʌ, æ, ɜː, ə, e, eɪ, ɪ, i. In the sentence below, all of these 'vowel phonemes' are included. It's worth reading it aloud to feel the way the shape of your mouth changes from start to finish:

Who would know aught of art must learn, act, and then take his ease.

In addition, there are six more diphthongs, aɪ, aʊ, ɔɪ, ɪə, eə, ʊə, which are included in this sentence:

My sound choice clears their doors.

Such sentences are known as 'phonetic pangrams': they are similar to normal pangrams but aim to use a complete list of phonemes rather than letters. The sentence below includes all the consonant phonemes as well as the vowels:

> The hungry purple dinosaur ate the kind, zingy fox, the jabbering crab and the mad whale and started vending and quacking.

In all there are forty standard phonemes used in English, although when technicians record people's voices in order to create synthesized speech programs, they need to record many more than this in order to capture different inflections and slight differences in the way phonemes sound in different words.

A GRAMMAR NURSERY RHYME

This old poem is a nice way to remember the parts of speech:

> Every name is called a **noun**,
> As *field* and *fountain*, *street* and *town*.
> In place of noun the **pronoun** stands,
> As *he* and *she* can clap *their* hands.
> The **adjective** describes a thing,
> As *magic* wand and *bridal* ring.
> The **verb** means action, something done –
> To *read*, to *write*, to *jump*, to *run*.

How things are done, the **adverbs** tell,
As *quickly, slowly, badly, well.*
The **preposition** shows relation,
As *in* the street, or *at* the station.
Conjunctions join, in many ways,
Sentences, words, *or* phrase *and* phrase.
The **interjection** cries out, 'Hark!
I need an exclamation mark!'
Through poetry, we learn how each
Of these make up the **Parts of Speech**.

Also remember that a pronoun is a common word
that is a **pro** at taking the place of a **noun**.

PUNCTUATION

When learning or teaching punctuation, it can be
useful to give the student a visual image of each
punctuation mark, for instance:

Full stop – a small ball.

Comma – a tadpole.

Apostrophe – a floating tadpole.

Semicolon – a ball being launched off a ramp.

Colon – two balls.

Brackets – a boomerang.

Underscore – a diving board (because, if a person stood on the baseline, it would be under their feet).

Hyphen – a belt (because it would be halfway up a person standing on the baseline).

Double quotes – someone doing the finger mime for quotes.

Single quotes – two tadpoles.

COMMAS

The correct place to put a comma is not 'where you would naturally take a breath in a sentence' (although that isn't a terrible rule of thumb). They are often used to separate subordinate clauses, which are clauses that add information to a sentence and could thus be removed from the sentence without rendering it meaningless (to summarize a complex subject). For instance, in these sentences the italicized sections are subordinate clauses

Even though it had been boiled for hours, the meat was still tough.

Mike, *who was wearing a red shirt,* arrived at ten o'clock.

While Jimmy slept, the family dog chewed his homework diary.

A traditional poem that reminds you of the comma's purpose in such sentences is:

A cat has claws at the ends of its paws.
A comma's a pause at the end of a clause.

THE OXFORD OR SERIAL COMMA

There are, of course, other uses of commas. For instance, they can be used to separate items in a list. One of the nerdier obsessions of editors is the use of a comma after the penultimate item in a list. For instance, here is the same list with and without:

The colours of the rainbow are red, orange, yellow, green, blue, indigo, and violet.

The colours of the rainbow are red, orange, yellow, green, blue, indigo and violet.

The controversy arises because some people argue that the commas in sentences such as this are standing in for the word 'and' (or sometimes for the word 'or'), so using one before 'and' in the first sentence above is effectively a repetition. Others argue that the best way to avoid confusion is to always include it.

For instance, in this sentence, the omission of the comma in the second version arguably changes the meaning of the sentence:

I love my dogs, David Bowie, and Chelsea.

I love my dogs, David Bowie and Chelsea.

In the second version, it looks like the dogs are called David Bowie and Chelsea. You could deal with this by rewriting the sentence, with the dogs at the end of the list, but there is no need if you have the extra comma there. The extra comma in the first of each pair of sentences is called the Oxford comma in the UK and the serial comma in the USA. Regardless of where you stand on this issue, you can remember that:

In this sentence with an Oxford/serial comma, there is a comma after the first, second, and last items in a list.

PARAGRAPHS

It can be difficult to know when a new paragraph is appropriate in a piece of writing. Here is a little rhyme that can be turned to for advice:

Four 'T's, a little writing rhyme
Of Topic, Territory, Talker, Time
When there's a change in one of these
Start a new paragraph if you please.

EXCLAMATION MARKS

This poem, which comes from the seventeenth century, gives a rather arcane explanation of the use of exclamation marks:

> This stop denotes our Suddain Admiration,
> Of what we Read, or Write, or giv Relation,
> And is always cal'd an Exclamation.

DOUBLE NEGATIVES

Double negatives are sentences in which the use of two negative words cancels the meaning of both, for instance 'We **didn't** do **nothing**.' They are best avoided, other than in song lyrics, where they crop up surprisingly often, as in 'You **ain't** seen **nothing** yet' or 'I **can't** get **no** satisfaction'. To remember this rule, imagine someone you regard as a fool saying, 'I don't know nothing about double negatives.'

SWAG

When children start to create longer pieces of writing, it can help to have a mnemonic that reminds them of some of the basics of good writing: **SWAG** stands for:

- Start with a capital letter.
- Write neatly.
- A space between words.
- Give punctuation at the end of sentences.

Or you can use **CUPS** for **C**apitalization, **U**sage, **P**unctuation, **S**pelling. For the recommended steps of the writing and editing process (Pre-Write, Draft, Revise, Edit, Publish, Celebrate), you can remember that:

Pretty **D**olls **R**arely **E**ver **P**unch **C**ows.

POW AND TREE

When writing non-fiction, you might want to use these two mnemonics to remember the best approach. **POW** stands for:

- **P**ick an idea or opinion.
- **O**rganize your notes.
- **W**rite about the subject.

When it comes to the final stage, the writing, you can use **TREE**:

- **T**opic sentence – an introductory sentence giving a statement of your intentions.

- Reasons – give at least three or four reasons to support your statement.
- Explain your reasons – back up your reasons with further detail.
- Ending – finish with a paragraph or sentence that summarizes your points.

STORYTELLING

If, on the other hand, you are writing a story, here is a mnemonic to help you remember some important elements of storytelling:

Very Many Pupils Come To School.

It stands for Viewpoint, Mood, Plot, Characters, Theme, Setting.

COLUMBUS SAILED
THE OCEAN BLUE

World History

In this chapter, we'll take a look at ways to remember some key facts, names and dates from the history of the world.

CHINESE DYNASTIES

Here is a brief summary of the rulers of China, from 2205 BC onwards

- **Xia (Hsia)**, 2205 to 1766 BC
- **Shang**, 1766 to 1122 BC
- **Zhou (Chow)**, 1122 to 770 BC
- Spring & Autumn Annals, 770 to 476 BC
- Warring States, 476 to 221 BC
- **Qin (Chin)**, 221 to 206 BC
- **Han**, 206 BC to 220 AD
- Three Kingdoms, 220 to 265 AD

- **Jin (Tsin)**, 265 to 420 AD

- **Southern and Northern**, 420 to 589 AD

- **Sui**, 589 to 618 AD

- **Tang**, 618 to 907 AD

- Five Dynasties, 907 to 960 AD

- **Song (Sung)**, 960 to 1280 AD

- **Yuan**, 1280 to 1368 AD

- **Ming**, 1368 to 1644 AD

- **Qing (Ching)**, 1644 to 1911 AD

- Republic of China, 1911 to 1949 AD (and ROC in Taiwan after 1949)

- People's Republic of China (Mainland China), 1949 AD

The periods in bold are traditionally regarded as the thirteen dynasties of China. You can learn the list using the mnemonic below

She Shabbily **Cho**se **Chi**nese **Han**d **Ji**ngles & **Sou**lfully **Su**nny **Tan**go **Son**gs: '**You** & **Me**, **Chi**ckadee!

THE CRADLE OF CIVILIZATION

The 'fertile crescent' is the area of the Near East that today reaches the northern River Nile through Syria, and stretches down through Iraq to the Persian

Gulf. This was where some of the earliest civilizations developed in history, due to the combination of fertile agricultural land and mild conditions. If you want to remember the names of the Sumerian, Mesopotamian, Babylonian, Akkadian and ancient Egyptian cultures, you could use this mnemonic:

Summer **M**eans **B**aby **A**xes **E**ggs.

Or

Summer **M**eans **B**aby **A**rcade **E**xists.

(Picture a shopping arcade full of baby shops that only opens in the summer.)

GREEK MYTHOLOGY

The word mnemonic is derived from the Greek goddess of memory, Mnemosyne: she was one of the original twelve Titans, who were the children of Uranus and Gaia: the other females were Tethys, Theia, Phoebe, Rhea and Themis, while the males were Oceanus, Hyperion, Coeus, Cronus, Crius and Iapetus. If you want to remember their names then for the females you could use:

Madame **T**itans **T**ook **P**owerful **R**oles **T**ogether.

For the males:

Olympians Had Competition. Cronus Couldn't Impose.

The second sentence is reinforced by the fact that Cronus, who had overthrown their father Uranus, was himself overthrown by his children, the first generation of Olympians: Zeus, Hades, Poseidon, Hestia, Hera and Demeter.

Zeus Had Power: He Headed Deities.

THE RULERS OF ROME

Julius Caesar was part of the triumvirate that was in power in Rome from 60 BC, and became 'Dictator' of Rome in 49 BC. His successors were known as 'Emperor'. In order to remember the rulers of Rome from Julius up to Nero you can remember:

Just Another Tom Cat Caught Napping.

- ~ **Julius,** 49 to 44 BC
- ~ **Augustus,** 31 BC to 14 AD
- ~ **Tiberius,** 14 to 37 AD
- ~ **Caligula,** 37 to 41 AD
- ~ **Claudius,** 41 to 54 AD
- ~ **Nero,** 54 to 68 AD

THE BIRTH OF PHILOSOPHY

The Ancient Greeks gave us some of the most extraordinary thinkers of early civilizations, not to mention their many breakthroughs in mathematics, science and engineering. If you need to remember this chronological list of ten great philosophers, you can use the mnemonic below.

- Thales of Miletus, 620 to 546 BC
- Anaximander, 610 to 546 BC
- Pythagoras, 570 to 495 BC
- Parmenides, 560 to 510 BC
- Anaxagoras, 500 to 428 BC
- Empedocles, 490 to 430 BC
- Zeno, 490 to 430 BC
- Socrates, 469 to 399 BC
- Plato, 427 to 347 BC
- Aristotle, 384 to 322 BC

That **A**ngry **P**ython **P**arked **An** **E**mpty **Z**-Car, **S**mart **P**eople of **A**thens.

If you only need to remember the most important three philosophers, you could just stick to **S**mart **P**eople of **A**thens (or the more visual cue, **Soc**ks on a **Plat**e being eaten by an **Aristo**crat) for Socrates, Plato and Aristotle.

THE SIX SIMPLE MACHINES

Since antiquity (and at least since the Ancient Greeks) humankind has known of six 'simple machines', which are ways of multiplying the force that a human can apply: these are the Pulley, Gear, Jackscrew, Axle and Wheel, Inclined Plane and Lever, for which this acronym has been devised: **PG JAIL**.

THE LIFECYCLE OF THE ROMAN EMPIRE

In order to remember the dates usually given for the founding of Rome (625 BC) and the fall of its empire (476 AD), you could use a system that substitutes letters for numbers according to their position in the alphabet.

So 625 BC can be rendered as FBE BC, while 476 AD can be rendered as DGF AD. For the first date, use:

Founding **B**ig **E**mpire **B**efore **C**hristianity.

For the second, use:

Dammit: **G**reat **F**ailure **A**fter **D**ecline!

THE CRUSADES

In 1095, Pope Urban II called on Western countries to mount a 'holy' war to recapture the Holy Land, thus triggering decades of conflict – his call led directly to the First Crusade. This mnemonic uses the number of letters in each word (bearing in mind that ten letters indicates a zero) to record the date: imagine the Pope saying,

A Suggestion: Jerusalem Saved.

THE BLACK DEATH

The Black Death was at its peak in Europe from 1347 to 1351. To remember the first of those dates, use this bubonic mnemonic, which gives the date through the number of letters in each word:

A Bad Dark Illness.

To remember both dates, you can turn it into a couplet – the first line gives the date, the second the duration:

A Bad Dark Illness,
Four Years of Death.

THE COPERNICAN REVOLUTION

Nicolaus Copernicus is famous for the publication of *De revolutionibus orbium coelestium* in 1543: this led to the Copernican Revolution, in which the theory that the Earth was the centre of the universe was finally shown to be incorrect. To remember the date, you can use this rhyme:

> In fifteen forty-three,
> To the shock of everyone,
> Copernicus decreed
> The Earth turned round the sun.

THE HISTORY OF THE US

Early in the twentieth century, the American poet and child prodigy Winifred Sackville Stoner Jr was concerned about the pernicious influence of nursery rhymes on young minds, and believed that she could address this by writing worthier rhymes with educational purposes. Her most famous poem, 'The History of the US', starts with these well-known lines on Christopher Columbus's 'discovery' of the New World in 1492

> In fourteen hundred, ninety-two,
> Columbus sailed the ocean blue.

And found this land, land of the Free,
beloved by you, beloved by me.

(Of course we now know that Columbus was beaten by many centuries by the Vikings, who had a settlement there in about 1000 AD, but Columbus's journey remains a significant moment in history as it led to the much greater level of European colonization in subsequent centuries.)

It's worth looking up the whole poem, but another entertaining section deals with the War of Independence:

In seventeen hundred seventy-five,
Good Paul Revere was then alive;
He rode like wild throughout the night,
And called the Minute Men to fight.
Year seventeen hundred seventy-six,
July the fourth, this date please fix
Within your minds, my children dear,
For that was Independence Year.

AMERICAN PRESIDENTS

The first seven Presidents of the USA were:

- George **W**ashington (1789–97)
- John **A**dams (1797–1801)

- Thomas **J**efferson (1801–9)
- James **M**adison (1809–17)
- James **M**onroe (1817–25)
- John Quincy **A**dams (1825–9)
- Andrew **J**ackson (1829–37)

Washington **A**nd **J**efferson **M**ade **M**any **A**rtful **J**udgements.

The twentieth-century Presidents were:

- Theodore **R**oosevelt (1901–9)
- William H. **T**aft (1909–13)
- Woodrow **W**ilson (1913–21)
- Warren **H**arding (1921–3)
- Calvin **C**oolidge (1923–9)
- Herbert **H**oover (1929–33)
- Franklin **D**. **R**oosevelt (1933–45)
- Harry S. **T**ruman (1945–53)
- Dwight **E**isenhower (1953–61)
- John F. **K**ennedy (1961–3)
- Lyndon B. **J**ohnson (1963–9)
- Richard **N**ixon (1969–74)
- Gerald **F**ord (1974–7)
- Jimmy **C**arter (1977–81)
- Ronald **R**eagan (1981–9)
- George H. W. **B**ush (1989–93)
- William J. **C**linton (1992–2001)

Here's a mnemonic (using 'FDR' to distinguish the two Roosevelts):

> **R**oosevelt **T**akes **W**ilson's **H**and,
> **C**oolly **H**oovering **FDR**'s **T**rue **E**xperiences.
> **K**ennedy, **J**ustly **N**oted **F**or **C**andour,
> **R**ead **B**ooks **C**arefully.

AMERICAN STATES

> **M**y **N**ice **N**ew **C**ar **N**eeds **R**e-**P**ainting. Maybe **D**ark **V**iolet? **N**o **S**hiny **G**old!

This acrostic is a help when it comes to remembering the original thirteen states of the United States of America: **M**assachusetts, **N**ew Hampshire, **N**ew York, **C**onnecticut, **N**ew Jersey, **R**hode Island, **P**ennsylvania, **M**aryland, **D**elaware, **V**irginia, **N**orth Carolina, **S**outh Carolina and **G**eorgia. It might also help to remember that among those 'N's there are three 'New's and a 'North'.

If you are studying the lead-up to the American Civil War then this sentence can help you remember the order in which states seceded from the Union:

> **S**o **M**y **F**ather **A**te **G**rapes **L**ast **T**uesday, **V**ery **A**wesome **T**art **N**apas [or **V**ery **A**wesome & **T**erribly **N**ice].

It stands for: **S**outh Carolina, **M**ississippi, **F**lorida, **A**labama, **G**eorgia, **L**ouisiana, **T**exas, **V**irginia, **A**rkansas, **T**ennessee and **N**orth Carolina.

THE FRENCH REVOLUTION

Here's a handy way to remember the main causes of the French Revolution in 1789: **MEAT**. This stands for:

- **M**onarchy: Louis XVI and his wife Marie Antoinette were deeply unpopular with their subjects.
- **E**nlightenment ideals: in the Age of Enlightenment new ideas were circulating, including natural rights and the social contract.
- **A**merican Revolution: the French people knew that the Americans had risen up against monarchy and prevailed, and this encouraged them to try the same.
- **T**axes: the expensive lifestyle of the monarch and the costs of fighting the Americans were funded by cripplingly high taxes, which were paid only by the third estate (the peasants and bourgeoisie) in France.

PROHIBITION IN THE USA

The sale of alcoholic beverages was illegal in the United States between 1920 and 1933:

Before nineteen twenty
There was drinking aplenty

Until nineteen thirty-three
It was juice, coffee or tea.

THE WALL STREET CRASH

The Great Depression of the 1930s was partially triggered by the Wall Street Crash in 1929. This is a letter-counting phrase to remember the date:

A ruination of economics.

UNITED NATIONS DECLARATION OF HUMAN RIGHTS

If you want to remember the date of the United Nations Declaration of Human Rights use this mnemonic, in which the number of letters in each word records the year of 1948:

A Peaceable Kind Covenant [or, if you prefer, Contract].

THE SPACE RACE

Here's a very brief history of the space race: in 1957, the Russian dog Laika was the first animal to orbit the earth; in 1959, the Russian probe Luna 2 collided with the surface of the moon; in 1961, Yuri Gagarin was the first man to reach outer space; and, finally, Neil Armstrong became the first man to set foot on the moon, during the Apollo 11 mission in 1969:

Laika in fifty-seven, Luna 2 in fifty-nine,
Gagarin in sixty-one, Armstrong in sixty-nine.

CAMELS ORDER SILVER DEVICES

Science and Astronomy

Learning about science involves trying to remember a lot of jargon and lists, for which mnemonics can be extremely useful. This chapter is a cornucopia of scientific shortcuts.

THE SCIENTIFIC METHOD

Here's a quick mnemonic for remembering the order and stages of the scientific method:

Quickly **R**un **H**ome **E**ating **C**urried **R**adishes.

First you **question**, then you do your **research**. You come up with a **hypothesis**, and carry out **experiments** to test it. Finally, you come to a **conclusion** and write up your **report**.

GEOLOGICAL TIME PERIODS

When classifying rocks and fossils, scientists use the following set of periods:

- Cambrian, 570 to 510 million years ago (mya)
- Ordovician, 510 to 439 mya
- Silurian, 439 to 409 mya
- Devonian, 409 to 363 mya
- Carboniferous, 363 to 290 mya
- Permian, 290 to 245 mya
- Triassic, 245 to 208 mya
- Jurassic, 208 to 146 mya
- Cretaceous, 146 to 65 mya
- Palaeocene, 65 to 56.5 mya
- Eocene, 56.5 to 35.4 mya
- Oligocene, 35.4 to 23.3 mya
- Miocene, 23.3 to 5.2 mya
- Pliocene, 5.2 to 2.5 mya

A good mnemonic for remembering the first four of these periods is:

Camels **Ord**er **Sil**ver **Dev**ices.

If you want to remember the whole list, then you can use this series of phrases (try to come up with a visual image for each line):

Camels **Ord**er **Sil**ver **Dev**ices,

Careful **Per**son **Tri**cks **Jur**y,

Creepy **Pal**ace Echoes,

Oliver's **Mi**niature **Pli**nth.

This has the first three letters of each period except for 'Echoes', which does contain 'e', 'o' and 'c', albeit in the wrong order, and 'Miniature', for which you at least have the hint of **Mi**ocene and **Pli**ocene being similar words.

LEARNING THE ELEMENTS

The first ten elements are: Hydrogen, Helium, Lithium, Beryllium, Boron, Carbon, Nitrogen, Oxygen, Fluorine and Neon. Here's an alternative version of the mnemonic on page 18:

Herbert Hoover Liked Booze But Could Not
Overcome Flatulent Nights.

For the next eight elements, Sodium, Magnesium,
Aluminium, Silicon, Phosphorus, Sulfur, Chlorine
and Argon:

Saucy Magpies Always Sing Perfect Songs
Clawing Ants.

The commonest magnetic elements are Nickel, Iron,
Copper and Steel, which can be remembered with:

Never Iron Creased Shirts.

Alternatively, if you are confident of your chemi-
cal symbols (such as H for Hydrogen and He for
Helium), you can use this version for the first twenty
elements.

Hi!	H
He	He
Lies	Li
Because	Be
Boys	B
Can	C
Not	N
Operate	O
Fireplaces	F
New	Ne
Nation	Na

Might	Mg
Also	Al
Sign	Si
Peace	P
Security	S
Clause	Cl
A	Ar
King	K (Potassium)
Can	Ca (Calcium)

THE EARTH'S ATMOSPHERE

The atmosphere of the Earth is made up of a series of layers: Troposphere, Stratosphere, Mesosphere, Thermosphere and Exosphere. You can use one of these mnemonics to remember these:

The Strong Man's Triceps Explode.

Troublesome Student's Messy Thermal Explosions.

CLASSIFICATION OF SPECIES

When classifying species, the following taxonomic ranks are used: Domain, Kingdom, Phylum, Class, Order, Family, Genus and Species. You can remember this with:

Dreadful **K**ing **P**hilip **C**ame **O**ver **F**rom **G**reat **S**pain.

Or, if you prefer a ruder version:

Dirty **K**nickers & **P**ants **C**ome **O**ff **F**or **G**reat Sex.

For the specific taxonomy of the human species, which is Animalia, Chordata, Mammalia, Primate, Hominidae, *Homo sapiens*, you could use one of these lines:

All **C**ool **M**en **P**refer **H**aving **H**eavy **S**ideburns.

Anyone **C**an **M**ake **P**retty **H**earty **H**ot **S**tew.

BIOLOGY

The ABC of an environment is **A**biotic, **B**iotic and **C**ultural: within a natural environment. Abiotic means non-living, biotic means living, and cultural means man-made.

MITOSIS

To remember the stages of mitosis (cell division), which are Interphase, Prophase, Metaphase, Anaphase and Telophase, you have a few choices of mnemonic:

I Picked **M**y **A**pples **T**oday.

I Propose **M**en **A**re **T**oads.

Idiot, **P**ass **M**e **A**nother **T**equila.

THE TWO TYPES OF CAMEL

The Dromedary camel, which has one hump, starts with a D. The Bactrian camel, which has two humps, starts with a B. Remember the number of humps in capital 'D' and 'B' to remember which has the most humps.

THE SOLAR SYSTEM AND THE STARS

Mnemonics for the order of the planets in the solar system used to include nine planets, Mercury, Venus, Earth, Mars, Jupiter, Saturn, Uranus, Neptune and Pluto. So, for instance, you could use:

My **V**ery **E**ducated **M**other **J**ust **S**erved **U**s **N**ine **P**ies.

My **V**ery **E**asy **M**ethod: **J**ust **S**et **U**p **N**ine **P**ies.

My **V**ery **E**asy **M**emory **J**ingle **S**eems **U**seful **N**aming **P**lanets.

Since 2006, however, Pluto is no longer regarded as a planet (just as a 'dwarf planet'), so shorter, eight-planet versions are now required, such as:

My Very Energetic Mother Just Sends Us Nuts.

Some enterprising scientists and authors have also found ways to protest about the bad treatment meted out to Pluto:

Many Very Educated Men Justify Stealing Unique Ninth.

Many Very Erudite Men Just Screwed Up Nature.

My Very Easy Memory Jingle Seems Useless Now.

Alternatively, you might want to remember not only the planets and the dwarf planet Pluto, but also four other dwarf planets that have been given the same ranking as Pluto in recent years: Ceres, Makemake, Haumea and Eris.

My Very Educated Mother Cannot Just Serve Us Nine Pizzas – Hundreds May Eat!

Another traditional astronomy mnemonic records the brightest stars in the sky:

Sir Can Rig A VCR, Pa!

This stands for: **Sir**ius in Canis Major, **Can**opus in Carina, **Rig**il Kentaurus in Centaurus, **A**rcturus in Boötes, **V**ega in Lyra, **C**apella in Auriga, **R**igel in Orion, **P**rocyon in Canis Minor and **A**chernar in Eridanus.

Walt Whitman's poem 'When I Heard the Learn'd Astronomer' is not a mnemonic device, but it is worth including here as a reminder that dry theorems and lists are no match for direct observation of the wonders of the universe:

When I heard the learn'd astronomer,
When the proofs, the figures, were ranged in
    columns before me,
When I was shown the charts and diagrams, to
    add, divide, and measure them,
When I sitting heard the astronomer where he
    lectured with much applause in the lecture-
    room,
How soon unaccountable I became tired and sick,
Till rising and gliding out I wander'd off by myself,
In the mystical moist night-air, and from time to
    time,
Look'd up in perfect silence at the stars.

THE PROPERTIES OF MATTER

The fundamental properties of matter are: Mass, Density, Volume and Weight, for which you can use this mnemonic:

Monkeys **D**ance **V**ery **W**ell.

COMPUTING

To remember the seven layers of the OSI (Open Systems Interconnection) model (which are Physical, Data Link, Network, Transport, Session, Presentation and Application):

Please **D**o **N**ot **T**hrow **S**ausage **P**izza **A**way.

Or, in reverse order:

All **P**eople **S**eem **T**o **N**eed **D**ata **P**rocessing.

HOW HARD ARE YOU?

The Mohs hardness scale is used to measure how hard a mineral or rock is: essentially the harder rock will scratch a softer rock, and the following minerals are used as benchmarks for the levels 1 to 10: Talc, Gypsum, Calcite, Fluorite, Apatite, Orthoclase feldspar, Quartz, Topaz, Corundum, Diamond.

Toronto **G**irls **C**an **F**lirt **A**nd **O**ther **Q**uirky **T**hings **C**an **D**o.

CHEMISTRY

Hydrocarbons are compounds in which carbon and hydrogen atoms are joined together by covalent bonds. If they have a single bond and are saturated, they are **alkanes**, while a double bond is found on an unsaturated **alkene**. To remember the alkenes (Methane, Ethane, Propane, Butane, Pentane, Hexane):

> **M**y **E**normous **P**enguin **B**ounces **P**retty **H**igh.

OXIDATION AND REDUCTION

Another traditional mnemonic spotlights the difference between **oxidation** (the loss of electrons from a substance) and **reduction** (the gain of electrons by a substance) – **OIL RIG**: **O**xidation = **I**t **L**oses, **R**eduction = **I**t **G**ains.

THE HUMAN BODY

Medical students and fully qualified doctors both make extensive use of some traditional mnemonics that help them to remember lists of names. For instance **MRS GREN** is a shortcut for remembering the vital signs of life: **M**ovement, **R**espiration,

Sensitivity, Growth, Reproduction, Excretion, Nutrition.

In some lists, 'Sensitivity' is replaced by 'Irritability', in which case you can use **RINGMER** instead.

There are twenty amino acids in the proteins in your body. Your body synthesizes the 'nonessential' amino acids, but the 'essential' amino acids need to come from your diet: Phenylamine, Valine, Threonine, Tryptophan, Isoleucine, Methionine, Histidine, Arginine, Leucine and Lysine. The traditional mnemonic for this is:

Pvt. Tim Hall.

(Bear in mind that 'Pvt.' can be used as an abbreviation for Private, so imagine a soldier of lowly rank called Tim Hall.)

The cerebral cortex in the brain contains four section or lobes, Frontal, Parietal, Occipital, Temporal:

First Place Often Trounces.

For the nerves of the eye, Olfactory, Optic, Oculomotor, Trochlear, Trigeminal, Abducens, Facial, Acoustic, Glossopharyngeal, Vagus, Spinal Accessory and Hypoglossal:

On Old Olympus's Towering Tops, A Finn And German Viewed Some Hops.

For the bones of the leg, **H**ip, **F**emur, **P**atella, **T**ibia, **F**ibula, **T**arsals, **M**etatarsals and **P**halanges:

Help **F**ive **P**olice **T**o **F**ind **T**en **M**issing **P**risoners.

For the bones of the upper arm, **S**capula, **C**lavicle, **H**umerus, **U**lna, **R**adius, **C**arpals, **M**etacarpals and **P**halanges:

Some **C**rooks **H**ave **U**nderestimated **R**oyal **C**anadian **M**ounted **P**olice.

For the bones of the wrist, **N**avicular, **L**unate, **T**riquetrum, **P**isiform, **M**ultangular Greater, **M**ultangular Lesser, **C**apitate and **H**amate:

Never **L**ick **T**illy's **P**opsicle, **M**other **M**ight **C**ome **H**ome.

For the spinal column, from top to bottom the vertebrae are: **C**ervical, **D**orsal, **L**umbar, **S**acrum and **C**occyx:

Clever **D**ick **L**icks **S**ticky **C**ream.

Or, for those who call the dorsal the 'thoracic':

Canned **T**una **L**ooks **S**o **C**ramped.

More fun can be had with the many versions of the spiritual song 'Dem Bones'. If you substitute the bracketed words, the song doesn't scan as well, but is at least medically correct:

Dem bones, dem bones, dem dry bones,
The toe bone's [phalanx] connected to the foot
　　bone [metatarsal],
The foot bone's [metatarsal] connected to the ankle
　　bone [talus],
The ankle bone's [talus] connected to the leg bones
　　[tibia and fibula],
The leg bones're [tibia and fibula] connected to the
　　knee bone [patella],
The knee bone's [patella] connected to the thigh
　　bone [femur],
The thigh bone's [femur] connected to the hip bone
　　[innominate bone],
The hip bone's [innominate bone] connected to the
　　back bone [vertebral column],
The back bone's [vertebral column] connected to
　　the shoulder bone [scapula],
The shoulder bone's [scapula] connected to the
　　neck bone [vertebral column],
The neck bone's [vertebral column] connected to
　　the head bone [skull],
Next you've gotta add the arm bone [humerus],
Then you've gotta add the wrist bones
　　[radius and ulna],
Then you've gotta add the hand bones [metacarpals],
Then you've gotta add the finger bones [phalanges],
Then you've gotta add the rib bones [ribcage],
Doin' the skeleton dance.

For the ten systems of the human body, you can use **NICER DRUMS**, which stands for **N**ervous, **I**ntegumentary, **C**irculatory, **E**ndocrine, **R**espiratory, **D**igestive, **R**eproductive, **U**rinary, **M**uscular and **S**keletal.

The excretory organs of the body, **S**kin, **K**idneys, **I**ntestines, **L**iver and **L**ungs, are **SKILL**.

The signs of heart failure are **ABCDE**: **A**cidosis, **B**lue skin, **C**old skin, **D**ilated heart and **E**dema (known as Oedema in the UK):

Always **B**e **C**hecking **D**ouble **O**rders.

EVERY GOOD BOY DESERVES FUN

Music and Art

MUSICAL KEYS

The traditional mnemonic for remembering the order in which notes are sharpened as you move up through the keys is:

Father Charles Goes Down And Ends Battle.

After the key of C, which has no sharps, the key of G has one sharp, which is F; the key of D has two sharps, F and C; the key of A has three sharps, F, C and G, and so on. One advantage of this version is that it can be reversed to give the order in which notes are flattened

Battle Ends And Down Goes Charles Father.

A musical purist might argue that you don't need a mnemonic for this – so long as you know F is the first sharp, you can simply count four places up a looping alphabet from A to G (and vice versa for the flats):

F G A B C D E F G A B C D E F G A B C D E F
G A B

Many, however, will prefer a more visual method to this theoretical approach. My objection to the traditional version is a different one – that it is a bit dated and dull. I prefer the more amusing version suggested by a friend:

Father Christmas Gave Dad An Electric Blanket.

Blanket Exploded And Dad Got Cold Feet.

STRINGED INSTRUMENTS

Beginners on stringed instruments that need to be tuned often need a mnemonic for the correct tuning. For a guitar, the usual tuning is **EADGBE** from the lowest string in tone. To remember this you can use:

Elephants And Donkeys Grow Big Ears.

There are alternative versions for different tastes. For instance, a sci-fi and fantasy geek might prefer:

Elves And Dwarves Gather Before Elrond.

I prefer the version below as it seems ideal for ageing rockers and their beloved guitars:

Every **A**ble **D**ad **G**oes **B**ald **E**ventually.

The ukulele has the same top four strings as a guitar (DGBE) although the D is a higher tone than the G, rather than lower. The traditional way of remembering this is a bit different: the phrase 'My Dog Has Fleas' sung to the tune of the strings played in order is peculiarly catchy and easy to remember.

My dog has fleas, oh   yes, he does.   My dog has fleas that bite and buzz.

Violins and cellos can be tuned by remembering the bottom note and counting five notes forward for each subsequent note. The cello tuning is **CGDA**, while the violin is **GDAE**. But there are, of course, some mnemonics available. For instance, for violin we have:

Good **D**ogs **A**lways **E**at.

Great **D**eeds **A**re **E**xhausting.

Green **D**ust **A**llows **E**cstasy.

Grin **D**aily **A**nd **E**xhale.

I haven't seen as many variations for the cello, but I do like the weirdness of this common one:

Chickens **G**ive **D**ucks **A**cid.

THE CLEFS

The lines on the treble clef, **EGBDF**, have traditionally been remembered with:

Every **G**ood **B**oy **D**oes **F**ine.

The spaces can be directly remembered with the word **FACE**.

For the bass clef, **GBDFA**, use the slightly amended:

Good **B**oys **D**o **F**ine **A**lways.

And, for the spaces:

All **C**ows **E**at **G**rass.

A visual aid to remembering where the Cs are on the two clefs is this symmetrical image (which also adds the Fs and Gs):

MUSICAL MODES

Modes in music are variations on keys, which create different moods. A standard C major scale is CDEFGABC with no flats or sharps. Here is a list of how the different modes would affect a C scale:

- Ionian: This is exactly the same as a C major scale.

- Dorian: To get the Dorian mode, you need to use E and B flat. This is similar to the usual minor scale, although that would have an A flat as well (depending on what form of minor scale you were playing).

- Phrygian: The Phrygian mode has four flats, DEAB. This scale can often be heard in flamenco music.

- Lydian: The Lydian mode has just one sharp, F sharp.

- Mixolydian: This has just one flat, B flat. It can often be heard in popular music where the flattened seventh note is more common.

- Aeolian: This is the standard minor scale with E flat, A flat and B flat.

- Locrian: This has five flats: DEGAB.

A good way to understand the modes is to find the natural major scale for the pattern of flats or sharps, and then use the list of modes to count through the scale. To explain this, a B major scale would have five sharps B, C#, D#, E, F#, G#, A#, B. So the Ionian mode with five sharps starts on B. The same set of notes would make up the Dorian mode starting on C#, the Phrygian mode starting on D#, the Lydian mode starting on E, the Mixolydian mode starting on F#, the Aeolian (or natural minor) mode starting on G# and the Locrian mode starting on A#. You can remember the correct order for counting through the scale using the mnemonic below:

Insomniac Dolly Parton Likes Music A Lot.

THE ELEMENTS OF DESIGN

When it comes to artists, the seven elements of design are Shape, Texture, Colour, Form, Value, Space and Line. You could use one of these mnemonics to recall the list:

Sally Tried Colouring For Value So Lightly.

Shaggy Texans Collude For Value Spanish Lingerie.

THE PRINCIPLES OF DESIGN

The traditional seven principles of design are Unity, Contrast, Rhythm, Movement, Pattern, Balance and Emphasis:

> **U**nder **C**astles' **R**amparts **M**ay **P**eace **B**e **E**ngineered.

Or, in a different order

> **C**razy **P**erry **E**ats **B**ananas **R**andomly **U**nder **M**oonlight.

THE PRINCIPLES OF ARCHITECTURE

The Roman architect Vitruvius wrote the treatise *De Architectura*, which suggested three principles of good architecture:

- Firmitas (Durability) – a building be robust and long-lasting.
- Utilitas (Utility) – it should successfully fulfil its intended function.
- Venustas (Beauty) – it should be beautiful and uplifting to see.

You could remember **DUB**:

> **D**ucks **U**nder **B**ridges.

FACE, ARM, SPEECH, TIME

First Aid and Emergencies

Some mnemonics can literally be lifesavers: we've seen how medics use them to memorize parts of the body, but they also come in useful in accidents, medical emergencies and diagnoses, when remembering the key information quickly can make all the difference.

FAST

FAST is a mnemonic to help people to quickly identify the first indications of a stroke. It stands for:

- **F**acial drooping: if a section of the face, in particular one side, is drooping and partially immobile, or if the person has a crooked smile, this is one warning sign.

- **A**rm weakness: can they raise their arm fully, or are they having difficulty doing so?

- **S**peech difficulties: a person in the early stages of a stroke may find it hard to speak or to understand speech.

- **T**ime: if any or all of the symptoms above are spotted, it is important to move quickly and to call the emergency services.

HEART ATTACK SYMPTOMS

It can also be crucial to spot the immediate effects of a heart attack: These can be remembered with **SHARP PAIN**:

- **S**udden dizziness or faintness.

- **H**ot and profuse sweating.

- **A**shen skin and blue lips.

- **R**apid, irregular or weak pulse.

- **P**ersistent vice-like chest pain.

- **P**ain does not ease when the person rests.

- **A**ir hunger – are they gasping for air?

- **I**ndigestion – discomfort high in the stomach.

- **N**ormal breathing lost – in other words, breathlessness.

DR ABC

When first assessing a casualty victim, many doctors use the acronym **DR ABC** to remember the essential steps:

- **D**anger (check for any dangers to yourself or others).
- **R**esponse (check that the patient is responding).
- **A**irway (check the airway is clear).
- **B**reathing (look, listen and feel for breathing).
- **C**irculation (if need be, start CPR compressions and call for immediate assistance).

Alternatively, you can use the more complicated **DRS ABCD**. In this version **S** is for 'Send for help or call an ambulance', while **D** is for 'Defibrillator – apply if available'.

DEALING WITH A FIRE

If you discover a fire, **FIRE** is an acronym for the immediate steps you need to take:

- **F**ind the location of the fire.
- **I**nform people by shouting out or setting off alarms.
- **R**estrict the spread of fire.
- **E**vacuate the area or **E**xtinguish the fire.

(NB – only take the last two steps where it is safe to do so.)

If you need to use a fire extinguisher, then we can **PASS** on this simple set of instructions:

- **P**ull the pin.
- **A**im at the base of the fire.
- **S**queeze the trigger.
- **S**weep across the fire.

If you are on fire yourself then, as kids are often taught, you need to 'stop, drop and roll' to try and extinguish the flames.

REPORTING AN ACCIDENT

If you need to call the emergency services for help for yourself or others, remember **AMEGA** for the crucial steps:

- **A**ssess the overall situation.
- **M**ake the entire area safe.
- **E**mergency aid: offer where necessary.
- **G**et help.
- **A**ftermath.

MAJOR INCIDENTS

In the event of a severe incident, some emergency services use the acronym **METHANE**, which could also be useful if you are ever in the unfortunate position of needing to report a more serious accident:

- **M**ajor incident declared.
- **E**xact location of the incident.
- **T**ype of incident.
- **H**azards (present, potential and future).
- **A**ccess (how will emergency services reach the scene?).
- **N**umber, type and severity of casualties.
- **E**mergency services required.

When emergency services arrive on the scene, they also use **SAMPLE** as a way of remembering questions to ask and information to establish about casualties:

- **S**igns & symptoms.
- **A**llergies.
- **M**edication.
- **P**revious relevant medical history.
- **L**ast oral intake.
- **E**vent history.

The first three things they will check will often be the **Three Bs**: **B**reath then **B**lood (flow) then **B**ones.

They may also use **SOCRATES** for assessing pain:

- **S**ite – where is the pain?
- **O**nset – when did the pain begin?
- **C**haracter of the pain – is it sharp, dull or aching?
- **R**adiation – does the pain go anywhere else?
- **A**ssociated symptoms – are there any other symptoms such as nausea or vomiting?
- **T**iming – when did the other symptoms begin?
- **E**xacerbating and relieving factors – does anything make it better or worse?
- **S**everity – how bad is the pain on a scale of 0–10?

And for unconscious casualties, the acronym **FISH-SHAPED** is for remembering the main causes of unconsciousness:

- **F**ainting
- **I**nfantile convulsions
- **S**hock
- **H**ead injury
- **S**troke

- **H**eart attack
- **A**sphyxia (or **A**naphylaxis)
- **P**oisons
- **E**pilepsy
- **D**iabetes

Where a patient is in shock, you can remember the types of shock using the **R**oyal **N**avy **CHAMPS** range:

- **R**espiratory
- **N**eurogenic
- **C**ardiogenic
- **H**aemorrhagic
- **A**naphylactic
- **M**etabolic
- **P**sychogenic
- **S**eptic

In order to treat shock, you can use an old Scouting rhyme:

If he's red, raise his head
[for hypertension, heat stroke].
If he's pale, raise his tail [shock].
If he's blue, you have some breathing to do
[in other words, mouth-to-mouth resuscitation].

HYPERGLYCAEMIA AND HYPOGLYCAEMIA

To distinguish someone with excess sugar from someone with insufficient sugar, you can use this rhyme:

> Hot and dry,
> Sugar high;
> Cold and clammy,
> Need some candy.

DIAGNOSING HYPOTHERMIA

The 'umble' family of words gives us some of the more obvious symptoms of hypothermia: if the person is **fumbling**, **mumbling**, **stumbling** and **grumbling** then these are danger signs (though for some people, such as the current author, this could equally describe their behaviour any time they are woken too early in the morning).

FIRST AID FOR STRAINS

In case of a twisted ligament or muscle strain, you need some **RICE**:

- **R**est: encourage the patient to rest and to avoid unnecessary movement.

- **I**mmobilize the injured area to reduce pain and prevent further damage.

- **C**old: apply a cold pack to the injured area using ice or something cold such as a bag of frozen peas.

- **E**levate the injured area above heart level: this will reduce swelling (though take care in the case of more serious injuries as this could be unfeasible or too painful).

SAVING SOMEONE FROM DROWNING

Trying to save someone who is in trouble in the water can be a dangerous business. Some emergency services use the short rhyme

Reach, Throw, Row, Go

to remember the order of ways in which you should consider trying to help (although it is sometimes stressed that the first step should be check if it is possible to talk them to the shore/edge). The rhyme suggests the following order of priorities when assessing any rescue attempt:

- **Reach**: if the victim is close to the shore, edge or a boat, and is able to grab or can be grabbed, then the safest method may be to reach them with a pole, oar or outstretched arm.

- **Throw**: if the victim is too far away to be reached but conscious and can grab, then it may be possible to effect a rescue by throwing a rope or flotation device.

- **Row**: if the victim is too far from the shore or edge to be rescued using the strategies above, then the next option would be to find a safe boat in order to get close enough to reach them or throw them a line.

- **Go**: the last resort – if the victim is unconscious or can't be rescued by any of the means above as they are in too much trouble, then someone (only a strong swimmer and preferably only someone trained in lifesaving techniques in the water) may have to enter the water in order to assist them.

SURVIVING A TERRORIST ATTACK

The UK government's advice for your path of action if you are caught up in a terrorist attack is extremely simple, but worth knowing. It is simply

Run, Hide, Tell.

In other words, if there is a safe route, then run away. If there isn't a safe route, find somewhere to hide. And make sure you tell the authorities (and anyone you can safely contact in the area) about the danger.

SURVIVAL OUTLOOK

If you find yourself stranded or in a dangerous situation, it may be useful to know that a person in reasonable physical condition can expect to survive:

at least **three minutes** without air;

at least **three hours** without shelter (in adverse conditions);

at least **three days** without water;

at least **three weeks** without food (but with water and shelter).

These are all rough estimates, but they may be useful when it comes to prioritizing your needs.

ROAD SAFETY

One of the first mnemonics that drivers learn is **MSM** (which you might remember as the standard internet abbreviation of **M**ain**S**tream **M**edia):

- **M**irrors – check your mirrors (and over your shoulders if necessary) to assess the position and speed of traffic around you.
- **S**ignal – if necessary, signal to let other road users know what you are doing.
- **M**anoeuvre – a manoeuvre is a change in speed or direction.

The Manoeuvre part of this can be further broken down into **PSL**:

- **P**osition – make sure you take up the correct position for the manoeuvre you are undertaking.
- **S**peed – select the appropriate gear and speed for the manoeuvre.
- **L**ook – look to check it is safe to continue.

On motorways, drivers are advised to avoid being the 'meat in the sandwich'. This means that you should avoid being in the middle lane with vehicles to the left and right of you. The logic is that this gives you no room for an evasive manoeuvre if, for instance, the idiot lorry driver in the inside lane suddenly decides to pull into your lane without spotting you.

The Guild of Experienced Motorists advise **CAT** for good driving behaviour:

- **C**oncentrate on the road situation around you.

- **A**nticipate the actions of others (even the mistakes they might make).

- **T**olerate other drivers (rather than becoming aggressive or competitive).

Before you set out on any journey, the things you should check are **POWDERY**:

- **P**etrol (or other fuel) – do you have sufficient?

- **O**il – check the engine oil and other fluids.

- **W**ater – check coolant and windscreen reservoir and that the washer jets are clean and in good condition. Clean the windscreen if needed and don't forget antifreeze in winter.

- **D**amage – check for external damage, especially if your vehicle has been in a public place where someone may have collided with it.

- **E**lectrics – check that the lights are working in particular. You can use the reflection in nearby windows or car wings for this purpose.

- **R**ubber – check the tyres for pressure and depth of treads, and the condition of the wiper blades.

- **Y**ou – are you sure you are fit to drive and not too tired or in any other way impaired?

agreed between employee and employer should be **S**pecific, **M**easurable, **A**ttainable, **R**elevant and **T**imely.

SWOT ANALYSIS

Equally well known, **SWOT** analysis is a way of analysing a business model or a proposed business strategy. It stands for **S**trengths, **W**eaknesses, **O**pportunities and **T**hreats. At its simplest, it would involve taking a piece of paper or a whiteboard, dividing it into four quarters and then brainstorming the entries for each of the letters.

PERFECT PRESENTATION SKILLS

When it comes to making an effective presentation to a group of people, a scary thought for many of us, you can use the acronym **OSRAM**. It helps you remember **O**bjective, **S**peaker, **R**oom, **A**udience and **M**essage. These are the five different aspects of a presentation that you need to be clear about before you start.

Alternatively, you could remember the **Five Ps**: **P**roper **P**lanning **P**revents **P**oor **P**erformance. And, finally, if you are the speaker, you could also remember your **ABC** and make sure that you are **A**ccurate, **B**rief and **C**lear.

KISS

In a wide variety of business situations you need to communicate your message to colleagues or the wider world. A useful thing to bear in mind is the acronym **KISS**, which stands for **K**eep **I**t **S**imple, **S**tupid.

FAYOL'S PRINCIPLES OF MANAGEMENT

Henri Fayol was a successful mining executive in the nineteenth and early twentieth centuries: his fourteen Principles of Management were highly influential following their publication in 1916 and remain a useful summary of some of the most important morals that managers need to remember. They are:

- **D**ivision of Work
- **A**uthority
- **D**iscipline
- **U**nity of Command

- Unity of Direction
- Subordination of Individual Interests to the General Interest
- Remuneration
- Centralization
- Scalar Chain (the formal line of authority)
- Order
- Equity
- Stability of Tenure of Personnel
- Initiative
- Esprit de Corps

A mnemonic for remembering this long list is:

Divide All Duties Until Useless Stuff Remains, Choose Smart Officers, Even Sacking Incompetent Executives.

Alternatively, for the main roles of management you could just remember **PLOCS**: Planning, Leading, Organizing, Controlling, Staffing.

And here is a good mnemonic for business, **LEADERSHIP**:

- Listening: listen to everyone, from customers to managers and family and friends.
- Example: inspire other people by leading by example.

- **A**wareness: notice everything from the little details to the big picture.

- **D**evelopment: develop your own skills and those of your team.

- **E**xcellence: always do your best in all situations in the workplace.

- **R**esilience: don't be discouraged by setbacks.

- **S**tability: surround yourself with a good team and remember that a company with a high staff turnover is making an inefficient use of its staffing resources.

- **H**umility: bear in mind that humility is a strength.

- **I**nnovation: always encourage innovation from the top to the bottom of your company or department.

- **P**urpose: people are inspired at the workplace by the feeling they have a purpose and are appreciated.

MONOPOLY

In the world of economics, the acronym **SPEW** is a way of remembering the most important impacts of monopoly on an industry:

- **Service** – will lack of competition affect the consumer service?
- **Prices** – are the prices significantly higher than they would be in a competitive market?
- **Efficiency** – will the monopoly be productive and dynamic?
- **Welfare** – is there a loss of welfare in a market dominated by a monopoly?

SPICED, SLICED AND DICED

In the world of currency, a British person might remember **SPICED**:

Strong **P**ound,
Imports **C**heaper,
Exports **D**earer.

To adapt this for the US, we could use **S**liced and **DICED**:

Strong **D**ollar,
Imports **C**heaper,
Exports **D**earer.

INVESTORS

Investors often remember a few rhymes and sayings, for instance this first one gives a general indication of how interest rates affect the stock market:

> When rates are low
> Stocks will grow.
> When rates are high
> Stocks will die.

The well-known saying 'Sell in May and Go Away' refers to a perceived long-term phenomenon in markets whereby the returns in the May–October period are systematically lower than in the October–May period. (Although academics differ as to whether reality bears out this theory, and it is unclear whether it represents a genuine process of cause and effect or historical accident.)

The next two are not really mnemonics, just simple, catchy Warren Buffett quotes to remind investors of some crucial basics:

> Price is what you pay. Value is what you get.
>
> Rule No. 1: Never lose money. Rule No. 2: Never forget rule No. 1.

And when wondering whether to invest in a business you can also bear in mind the mnemonic **CAMPARI**:

- **C**haracter: is the business owner generally reliable and trustworthy?
- **A**bility: do they have the ability to deliver on their promises?
- **M**argin: what will the margin be on your investment?
- **P**urpose: to what purpose will they be putting the money?
- **A**mount: how much do you have to invest?
- **R**epayment: what are the repayment terms?
- **I**nsurance: do you have a way to arrange for security or insurance to guarantee the loan?

ELASTICITY OF SUPPLY

The ease with which supply can be increased or decreased in case of a change in demand for a product is known as 'elasticity of supply'. The acronym **BRITS** is a way to remember the main factors on elasticity of supply:

- **B**arriers to Entry: do patents or other high initial costs make it hard for new suppliers to enter the market?
- **R**aw Materials: how easily and quickly can more raw materials be obtained?

- **I**nventory: do businesses in the sector habitually hold high stock levels or not?

- **T**ime: agricultural products are an example of a product that can't be created in a hurry.

- **S**pare Capacity: the supply of goods and services is most elastic when there is plenty of spare labour and resources.

SALES MNEMONICS

The most important mnemonic rule for sales people is another **ABC**. This one means **A**lways **B**e **C**losing. The essential message is to keep in mind the final goal of closing a deal throughout the sales process.

It is also always wise to **PLAN** your sales strategies:

- **P**repare properly.

- **L**osing time loses the sale.

- **A**nalyse the situation.

- **N**ever just call (in other words, even a cold call needs a good reason).

Journalists and non-fiction writers are taught to remember the five 'W's and one 'H': **W**ho? **W**hen? **W**here? **W**hat? **W**hy? **H**ow? These are also useful to bear in mind in any sales call, trade fair or job interview as the overall narrative of how a deal will work will be predicated on the answers to these questions.

The **STAR** technique, which is usually suggested for interviewees trying to sell themselves, can also be used by salespeople:

- **S**ituation – if you are telling a story (for instance, in answer to the interview question, 'Tell us about an instance in which you took charge of a situation'), then firstly you need to take care to explain the basics of the situation in which you found yourself, and who else was involved.

- **T**ask – then you need to explain what task you were given or what challenge you faced (one alternative version of the mnemonic replaces **STAR** with **SCAR**, with the 'C' standing for **C**hallenge).

- **A**ctivity – explain what you actually did and how you fulfilled the task or took charge of the situation.

- **R**esult – and don't forget to conclude by explaining the outcome of the situation and your chosen course of action.

AIDA

For marketing and advertising, the goals in the age of social media and Snapchat are much the same as they were back in the days of billboards and early radio advertising. You need:

- **A**ttention (Attract It!)
- **I**nterest (Inspire It!)
- **D**esire (Create It!)
- **A**ction (Urge It!)

THE SPELLING BEE

Commonly Misspelled Words

English is a notoriously difficult language to learn, at least when it comes to the spelling and pronunciation of words.

So, for this final section of the book, let's look at a few of the mnemonics that can be used purely to remember the spellings of some of the English language's most commonly misspelled words. But first, there is a minor controversy to consider …

I BEFORE E EXCEPT AFTER C

This is the spelling rule that most people remember from school. It's also a rule that makes a lot of people angry once they realize how many exceptions there are to it.

You can patch up the original rule a bit if you add a second line as below:

I before E except after C,
When the sound is 'ee'.

This means that words such as 'science' where the 'i' follows the 'c' but the 'ie' isn't pronounced 'ee' are no longer exceptions to the rule. It also rules out troublesome words such as 'beige', or 'weight' for the same reason.

There continue to be exceptions, though, for instance:

~ 'Seize' and (arguably, depending on how you pronounce it) 'Weird'.

~ Proper names such as 'Leith' or 'Sheila'.

~ Some scientific words, including 'caffeine'.

~ Words that end in 'cy' such as 'legacy' for which the plural ends in 'cies': 'legacies'. (There are getting on for a thousand English words in this last category alone.)

So unfortunately, unless you want to learn the large list of outstanding exceptions, the rule is still fairly ineffective and the only way to be safe is to find mnemonics for words that you find troublesome. Some of these are included in the list of commonly misspelled words below.

ACCELERATE

Remembering that the phrase 'running at a good clip' is an archaic way to describe someone travelling at speed, then use this to remember the first three letters:

A Changing **C**lip.

Alternatively, note that there are two separate 'c' sounds, a hard 'c' followed by a soft 'c' sounding like an 's'.

ACCIDENTALLY

Similar to 'accelerate', there are two 'c' sounds (you could think of the way that 'x' is written for algebra, with two back-to-back curves, and remember that it takes two 'c's to make an 'x' sound). For the ending of the word, remember that:

I accident**ally** made an **ally**.

ACCOMMODATE/ ACCOMMODATION

The problematic part of these words is 'accomm' with a double 'c' and a double 'm'. Picture:

A **C**omfortable **C**ave **O**f **M**any **M**arvellous **O**rnaments.

AEROPLANE

For the first four letters remember:

All **E**ngines **R**unning **O**kay.

ALMOND

Remember that **al**monds are ov**al**-shaped.

APPARENT

It is *apparent* that this *app* was created for a picky *parent*.

(This mnemonic assumes you can work out for yourself that it is a bit unlikely to have three 'p's in a row ...)

ARGUMENTS

A Rowdy Girl's Underwear! **My Eyes Need Tied Shut!**

ARITHMETIC

A Rat In The House May Eat The Ice Cream.

ASSASSINATION

This can be made up of four words (including a double 'ass').

Ass, ass, I, nation.

ASTHMA

This can be caused by

A Sensitivity To Household Mites Arising.

BEAUTIFUL

The tricky bit in this word is 'beau': remember that:

Big **E**lephants **A**re **U**gly.

BECAUSE

This is another word where elephants, with their notoriously long memories, can help us out:

Big **E**lephants **C**an **A**lways **U**nderstand **S**mall **E**lephants.

BISCUIT

Bear in mind that:

BIScuits are **C**rumbled **U**p **I**nto **T**iny bits.

CALENDAR

The most common mix-up in this word is to replace the final 'a' with an 'e'. So remember that:

DARleen checked the calen**DAR** every **DA**y.

CARIBBEAN

This word is often misspelled with a double 'r' and single 'b'. Imagine a type of bean that comes from the Caribbean and is called the **Carib bean**.

CEMETERY

Imagine a squeamish class of children screaming 'e', 'e', 'e' in disgust as they walk past the graves.

CHURCH

CH on the right, **CH** on the left, and **U R** [you are] in the middle.

COMMITTEE

The inevitable laws of bureaucracy decree that:

Many **M**eetings **T**ake **T**ime & **E**veryone's **E**xhausted.

CONSCIENCE

Imagine a scientist who has doubts about the fake experiments he has been pretending to carry out:

The **con science** is weighing on his **conscience**.

DEFINITELY

Sometimes etymology is your friend: something is said to be definite if it is *definitus*, meaning within limits or 'with a **fini**sh' in Latin. 'Infinite' and 'finite' are related words meaning 'without limits' and 'with limits' respectively, and there is a **finite** in de**finite**.

DELIBERATE

This word can mean 'intentional' or, as a verb, 'to ponder or debate'.

A parole board deliberately deliberates whether or not to **liberate** a prisoner.

DESSERTS

Remember that:

> If you have several **desserts**, this is the opposite of being **stressed**.

DIFFICULTY

This is a rhyme that was featured by Roald Dahl in the wonderful book *Matilda*.

> Mrs D, Mrs I,
> Mrs FFI,
> Mrs C, Mrs U,
> Mrs LTY!

DILEMMA

To spell dil**emma**, you need an **Emma**.

DISAPPOINT

Commonly misspelled as 'disapoint'. Think of the saying 'two peas in a pod' and think how disappointing it would be to pick a peapod that only had two peas in it.

EMBARRASS

For this commonly misspelled word you can use:

Every **M**other's **B**oy **A**cts **R**ather **R**udely **A**fter **S**hameful **S**cenes.

Or, to remember the double letters:

When I'm embarrassed I go **R**osy **R**ed **A**nd **S**igh **S**adly.

ENVIRONMENT

The letter that is most often missed out is the 'n'.

Remember that a new env**iron**ment can **iron** you out.

EXAGGERATE

Here's a suitably ludicrous acrostic to help you remember how to spell **exaggerate**.

Excitement **A**s **G**rey **G**oats **E**at **R**ussian **A**ntelopes **T**his **E**vening.

FAMILIAR

This is an unusual spelling, often misspelled as 'familier'. Remember:

That **liar** looks fami**liar**.

(You can add your least favourite politician as a visual element if you want – I don't wish to incur a libel action by suggesting candidates.)

FLUORESCENT

This is a booby trap of a word, with two awkward letter combinations in 'uo' and 'sc'. It can be made of individual words, though:

Flu, ore, scent.

(Imagine a poor sick little gold nugget who has lost his sense of smell.)

FOREIGN

FOR Even In Great Nations places can seem foreign.

GENERALLY

A **general** is **generally** a good **ally**.

GOVERNMENT

This is another word where the etymology of the word is useful. It's very easy to forget the 'n' in this word, but if you remember that the **govern**ment **governs** it is easier to see why it is there (even though it is often not pronounced).

GRAMMAR

To avoid letting any rogue 'e's into this word, imagine your Grandma who has perfect grammar – both have 'a's but no 'e'.

GUIDANCE

The 'a' is confusing in this word, as the root word is 'guide'. Imagine a marriage gui**dance** counsellor who can **dance**.

HARASS

The most common mistake in spelling this word is a double 'r'. To remember the correct spelling, you could imagine an irritating dog harassing a hare, and notice that both 'harass' and 'hare' have a single 'r'. If you have trouble with the double 's', just think about where the hare might get bitten if it doesn't run away fast enough.

IMMEDIATE

This sentence helps with the parts of the word that are most often misspelled.

Mickey **M**ouse **ate imm**ediately.

INDEPENDENT

After the first letter, this word only needs 'e's for vowels. Remember that:

Trees only need 'e's because they are ind**e**pend**e**nt.

INDISPENSABLE

If an employee is truly **able** then they will be indispens**able**.

INTERRUPT

Remember that it is:

Really **r**ude to **interrupt**.

(And you should be able to remember the double 'r' that way.)

ISLAND

An **island is land** in the middle of the sea.

LIAISON

A liaison is a point of contact. You could imagine that the son of Li and Ai is their only contact after their divorce: **Li Ai son**. Alternatively, remember that if you use your two 'eyes' you will be able to see that it is correctly spelled.

MISSPELL

It would be particularly embarrassing to get the spelling of 'misspell' wrong. Remember that:

Miss Pell never **misspells**.

NECESSARY

The most common mistake here is including an unnecessary double 'c', although there are several other common misspellings:

Not **E**very **C**at **E**ats **S**ardines (**S**ome **A**re **R**eally **Y**ummy).

Or remember that:

It is **necessary** for a shirt to have one **C**ollar and two **S**leeves.

OCEAN

Only **C**lowns **E**at **A**t **N**oon.

(Imagine some clowns adrift on a raft in the ocean).

PARALLEL

The most common mistake in spelling this word is to forget where the double 'l' is. You could think of the word as a town with the railway tracks running through the centre.

PARLIAMENT

Remember that:

There is an 'I am' in Parl**iam**ent.

PSYCHOLOGY

Please **S**ay **Y**ou **C**an **H**it **O**ld **L**adies **O**r **G**et **Y**oghurt.

QUITE

Teachers have certain trigger words that can send them over the edge while marking children's writing: confusions of 'quiet' and 'quite' have been responsible for many private moments of meltdown, because:

> It is **Q**uite **U**nbelievably **I**mpossible **T**o **E**njoy marking misspelled writing.

RECOMMEND

Think of the easier word 'commend'. Recommend is simply 'commend' with 're' at the start of it.

RHYTHM

A weird-looking word that can be remembered with this neat acrostic:

> **R**hythm **H**elps **Y**our **T**wo **H**ips **M**ove.

SEPARATE

Think of a rat that has to be removed from its cage and quarantined from other rats: now there's **a rat** in a sep**arat**e container.

SIGNIFICANT

This can be made up of the words of a short sentence:

Sign, if I can't.

STAIR/STARE

Remember that:

You climb a st**air** into the **air**.

SUPERSEDE

When a word in English ends in the sound 'seed', it is almost always spelt 'cede' or 'ceed', as are 'concede' or 'proceed'. But true to form, the language has that one little word trying to catch you out: 'supersede' (meaning to discard or set aside), which ends in 'sede'. Imagine some wonderful seeds, such as the magic beans from which Jack grew his beanstalk. Then you just need to remember that you have to swap the last two letters to get from 'super seed' to 'supersede'.

TO/TOO

If you want to remember the spelling for 'too much' just remember which word has too many 'o's.

TRULY

Often misspelled as either 'truely' or 'truley', remember that:

It is tr**uly** hot in **July**.

VACUUM

This is an odd word because of the 'cuu' in the middle. You could use this mnemonic:

VAlerie **C**leans **U**p **U**gly **M**esses with a vacuum.

WEDNESDAY

Also known as:

We Do Not Eat Soup Day.

WHICH/WITCH

If you want to remember **which** of these words is **which**, remember that:

The w**itch** had an **itch**.

One of the irritations of the English language is that, because it has taken words from so many sources, from Latin to French to Anglo-Saxon to Viking and more, it has a bewildering variety of spellings, and there are also many words that are easy to confuse because they either sound the same or look the same. Just think of how different are the pronunciations for 'tough', 'bough', 'cough', 'dough', 'hiccough', 'thorough', 'lough' and 'through'. And there are many words such as 'bear' and 'bare' or 'cue' and 'queue' that sound exactly the same but mean different things. And that's not to mention words such as 'imply' and 'infer' that have related but subtly different meanings.

Let us look at a few ways to distinguish some of the most commonly confused words. You may not be able to remember all of these, but if there are particular words that you tend to get wrong, some of these hints may help.

ACCEPT/EXCEPT

If you **accept** something, you are agreeing to it. Both 'accept' and 'agree' start with an 'a'. **Except** is used to **ex**clude something – for instance, 'We were all wearing suits except Sally.' Both 'except' and 'exclude' start with 'ex'.

ADVICE/ADVISE

Advice is the noun, whereas to **advise** means to give a piece of advice or a recommendation. Remember that in 'a pie**ce** of advi**ce**' both words end in 'ce', whereas there is no such thing as 'a piece of advise'.

AFFECT/EFFECT

Outside of psychology textbooks, **affect** is a verb, describing the action of influencing something. For instance, 'Sad movies affect my mood negatively.'

Effect is a noun describing the result of such an action. A mnemonic for this is:

> The arrow affected the antelope. The effect was extraordinary.

Or you could use the mnemonic **RAVEN**:

> Remember: Affect, Verb; Effect, Noun.

ANTONYM/SYNONYM

Words that are **synonyms** mean the same thing (and same and synonym both start with 's'). **Antonyms** are words that mean the opposite to each other (antonym starts with 'ant', like 'anti', which also turns a word into its opposite).

BARE/BEAR

Both of these can have more than one meaning – **bare** can mean 'naked' or 'to expose', while a **bear** is a large mammal and 'to bear' means 'to carry'. Remember that a bear can bear a heavy load, while bare and expose both end in 'e'.

CENSOR/CENSURE

To **censure** is to criticize in strong terms, while to **censor** is to ban parts of a book, film or communication, and the **censor** is the person who does this. Remember that an auth**or** may be cens**or**ed by the cens**or**. And it will be the people who c**ensure** the book who **ensure** that this happens.

COMPLIMENT/COMPLEMENT

To **compliment** someone is to express approval (and a 'compliment' as a noun is a statement that does this), whereas to **complement** something is to add to it in a way that improves it. **I** give compl**i**ments, w**e** comple**ment** each other. And if we **comple**ment each other, you could even say that we **comple**te each other.

COUNCIL/COUNSEL

A **council** is a group of advisers or managers, while to **counsel** someone is to give them advice (and as a noun **counsel** simply means 'advice'). We associate coun**ci**ls with **ci**vic government and **ci**ties. For counsel you might remember the 's' by comparing the word to 'consult' or 'support'. Alternatively, you might note that if you are trying to **sell** someone an idea you might offer them coun**sel**.

CUE/QUEUE

First, here's a bit of trivia that may come in handy in a quiz sometime: there are only two words in the English language that have five or more vowels in a row: 'euouae', which is an archaic mnemonic to help singers remember a passage of medieval music, and 'queueing'. **Queue** is a pretty unusual word itself, a hangover from medieval French, which used to refer to 'tails' such as a chain of dancers or hair worn in a ponytail, but which is now mainly used to refer to a line of people or things waiting their turn. Some schools teach its spelling by pointing out how funny the spelling sounds when spoken aloud – 'Q, U-E, U-E!' You might like to picture the tail of the 'q' as a tail, or remember how many vowels are **queuei**ng up behind the 'q'. Alternatively, remember that a **cue** is a signal, prompt or hint, which is similar to a **clue**.

DISCREET/DISCRETE

These are two words with a tangled etymological history. If you are **discreet** you are being prudent and careful not to draw attention, while two things are **discrete** if they are separate and distinct. Imagine that the two 'e's are sharing a secret in 'discr**ee**t', while in 'discr**e**t**e**' they have been separated to prevent them from talking to each other.

ELICIT/ILLICIT

You **elicit** a reaction if you draw it out or provoke it, whereas an action is **illicit** if it is not allowed by the rules or the law. Bear in mind that **ill**icit and **ill**egal both start with 'ill'.

HOARD/HORDE

A **hoard** of gold coins or jam jars might be kept in a cupb**oard**, whereas a **horde** of people or animals is more like a crowd or large h**e**rd (and there is an 'e' in 'herd').

IMPLY/INFER

For word nerds, these two words are like a red rag to a bull, so if you really want to annoy your friendly local grammar pedant, feel free to use them incorrectly. If you would prefer to keep the peace, try to remember that they can be used to describe the same event in a slightly different way. If the author of a crime book **implies** that a character is the murderer, then they have suggested it or given the reader a hint that this is the case without explicitly saying so. If, however, the reader **infers** that this character is the murderer, then they have reached that conclusion themselves. It may help to know that 'imply' derives from the French word for folding (*plier*), which is also the root of **ply**wood or four-**ply** cashmere – when you imply something, you fold a meaning into your words.

LICENCE/LICENSE

A **licence** is a document granting permission, whereas you **license** someone to do something if you give them permission – in other words 'license' is a verb, but 'licence' is a noun. For one way of remembering the difference, see the section on 'practise' and 'practice' below. There is also a rhyme that some people use for this:

> S is the verb and C is the noun,
> That's the rule that runs the town.

PRACTICE/PRACTISE

Practise is a verb – Dr Foster practises medicine. **Practice** is a noun – the practice of selling snake oil is immoral and, in most states, illegal. Try remembering that 'noun' comes before 'verb' in the dictionary, and 'c' comes before 's' in the alphabet. (This is also an alternative way of telling 'advice' and 'advise' or 'licence' and 'license' apart.)

PRINCIPLE/PRINCIPAL

A **principle** is a fundamental rule or guideline. **Principal**, which means first in order of importance, can either be a noun or an adjective. You can remember that the princi**pal** is your **pal** (British readers would call a principal a headteacher but should be familiar with the language of American high schools from the many movies set there). As an adjective – 'he is the principal singer in the choir' – you can remember that principal has an 'a' (for adjective) in it.

STATIONARY/STATIONERY

Stationary means 'motionless' or 'still' (think of a car not moving, hence it is stationary), while **stationery** refers to writing materials (think of a pen lying on a desk, it is stationery, or you could also think of an envelope beginning with 'e' and therefore it being 'stationery').

Finally, since this whole book has been about them, here is a handy way to remember how to spell **mnemonic**:

Memorizers Need Easy Methods Of Noting Important Content.

And now you know that, you need never forget it again!

BIBLIOGRAPHY

There are many books on both memory and mnemonics in particular. I am grateful particularly to the titles and authors below:

Bryan, Roger, *It'll Come In Useful One Day* (Llanina Books, 2010)

Buzan, Tony, *The Memory Book* (BBC Active, 2009)

Chalton, Nicola, *Memory Power* (Magpie, 2006)

Hagwood, Scott, *Memory Power* (Free Press, 2007)

O'Brien, Dominic, *You Can Have An Amazing Memory* (Watkins Publishing, 2011)

Parkinson, Judy, *I Before E Except After C* (Michael O'Mara Books, 2011)

Parkinson, Judy, *Remember Remember, The Fifth of November* (Michael O'Mara Books, 2011)

Robledo, I. C., *Practical Memory* (CreateSpace, 2017)

ACKNOWLEDGEMENTS

———•◆•———

I'd like to thank Duncan Proudfoot, Al Barker, Vanessa Smith and Betsy Barker for suggesting particular rhymes or shortcuts that have been included in this book. Thanks as ever to the wonderful team at Michael O'Mara Books, in particular Louise Dixon for asking me to write this book and Gabby Nemeth for her meticulous editing. And, as ever, many thanks to my daughter and, above all, my wife for putting up with me.

INDEX

If you enjoyed *Never Eat Shredded Wheat,*
you'll love …

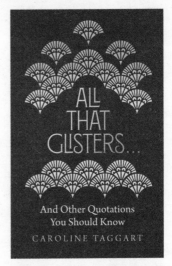

978-1-78243-988-2 in hardback format
978-1-78243-990-5 in ebook format

978-1-78243-997-4 in hardback format
978-1-78929-002-8 in ebook format